SELECTED CZECH TALES

SELECTED
CZECH TALES

Translated by
MARIE BUSCH
and
OTTO PICK

Short Story Index Reprint Series

BOOKS FOR LIBRARIES PRESS
FREEPORT, NEW YORK

First Published 1925
Reprinted 1970

INTERNATIONAL STANDARD BOOK NUMBER:
0-8369-3669-8

LIBRARY OF CONGRESS CATALOG CARD NUMBER:
73-132112

PRINTED IN THE UNITED STATES OF AMERICA

CONTENTS

PREFACE

I AM indebted to Mr Otto Pick for my introduction to and information concerning Czech literature as represented by the Short Story. He has endeavoured wholeheartedly and for many years to carry the interest in Czech literature beyond the confines of his own country, and to make Central and Western Europe, and the countries beyond the seas, realize the resurrection of a language which had been considered doomed for literary expression.

Indeed, for two centuries, the Czech language had been practically dead and buried. Bohemia suffered perhaps more severely than any other country in the Thirty Years' War, and after their defeat in the battle of the White Mountain in 1621, the Czech nation as such disappeared from European history. The country became an appendage of Austria; the Czech language was repressed. It subsisted in a rudimentary and shrunken form in the rural districts, the homely speech of illiterate peasants. By them the spark was kept glimmering under the ashes, and when a stronger racial and national feeling again began to assert itself a century ago, the devotees of Czech national expression turned a loving attention to this spark and fanned it with infinite care into a brighter glow.

The moving spirit of this resuscitation of the Czech literary language was a schoolmaster, Josef Jungmann. What Dr Johnson had done for the English language, Jungmann did for the Czech. Single-handed he carried out the enormous task of compiling a Dictionary of the Czech Language. But he had not the advantage that Johnson had of finding his subject ready and highly developed ; he had to collect the fragments of an impoverished and debased language, corrupted by the influx of foreign words. He recreated the pure Slav language from the old Czech literature which he unearthed, and from the peasants' vernacular; he tested its power and beauty and its fitness for expression of poetic thought by his translation of foreign classics. It is an interesting and remarkable fact that the work which practically accomplished this resur-

rection of the Czech language was Milton's
Paradise Lost, which Jungmann translated.
Published in 1811, it inaugurated the modern
movement towards fresh literary efforts.

Jungmann's call did not sound in vain. It
became evident that the genius of the country
had only been waiting for a medium in which
to express itself. The lyric and epic poems of
Mácha (1810-1836), and two decades later
those of K. Jaromír Erben, were the first
original works to emerge, and prose soon
followed. Two women writers, Božena
Němcová (1820-1862) and Karolína Světlá
(1830-1899), wrote novels depicting the life
of the Bohemian peasants, while Jan Neruda
(1834-1891) chiefly presented that of the
bourgeoisie in Prague. The same milieu
attracted Ignát Herrmann, whose delightful
sense of humour and human sympathy en-
deared him to his fellow-citizens and countrymen of pre-war imperial Prague, and still
makes this doyen of Czech novelists a favourite
in the newly created Republic.

The independence gained by the Czech
nation after the Great War has influenced the
mental attitude of its literary men, who feel
that they are now ranging themselves with the
writers of other European countries, and the

endeavour to command a wider outlook than
their national or local interests has made them
turn their attention more specially to the
literature of Western countries. Thus the
Brothers Čapek, whose plays are probably the
best known works of modern Czech literature
in this country, were influenced to some extent
by Mr H. G. Wells, while F. X. Šalda, the
leading literary critic, acknowledges his taste
to have been formed in the school of French
æsthetes such as Saint-Beuve and Taine, and
who applies their severe standards to his own
country's language, both in his own works
and in those of others. Distinct individuality
and strongly marked national features dis-
tinguish the work of each writer.

In this volume we present a number of
Czech Short Stories to English readers. The
scale on which it is planned allows only a
small selection: some writers, well known in
their own country, had to remain unrepre-
sented. All those included are acknowledged
to be of outstanding merit, and it is hoped
that a larger selection may at some future
time be possible. The more idealistic earlier
school is represented by Karolína Světlá,
Jan Neruda and Ignát Herrmann, while
the modern realistic movement finds more

marked expression in the two fanciful tales by
the Brothers Čapek, Josef (1887) and Karel
(1890), who are as remarkable for their gifts
of imagination and satire as for the harmonious
sympathy which joins their minds in their
work. Others included are Otakar Theer
(1885-1917), who unfortunately died too early
to fulfil all the hopes he had raised; K.
Čapek-Chod (1850), a powerful and earnest
novelist, whose understanding of the labouring
classes is expressed in the poignant story in
this book; F. X. Šalda (1868), who often
chooses a milieu other than that of his own
country, and Růžena Svobodová (1868-1920),
a woman writer whose thoughtful and indi-
vidual vision of life brings the volume to an
harmonious close.

                    MARIE BUSCH

A KISS

BY

KAROLINA SVĚTLÁ

THE midday bell had stopped ringing, and now it tolled. The children playing on the spacious green remained unconcerned; the men lifted their caps, but otherwise did not look as if anything special were happening; but the women—they did start! They all left what they were doing; one a half-cooked dinner, another the cows which she was just milking, the third her work in the store-room where she was getting rid of the winter's dust, after the fashion of good housewives, with the first warm rays of the sun. In short, from all their haunts and corners the curious daughters of Eve hurried to their usual place of assembly, the venerable centenarian lime tree that spread its huge, protecting arms over the plain little village church.

'Whoever can it be that has died so suddenly?' one neighbour asked of the other. But their astonished looks told plainly that none of them had had any idea of the

impending event.   No one had been known
to be dangerously ill.

Our good gossips make a guess in one or
the other direction, rack their brains in the
endeavour to find out the name of the deceased,
and make investigations concerning all the
inhabitants of the place. They do not fail
to fold their hands or to cross themselves
devoutly from time to time, so that the
wicked world should not say that it was
sinful curiosity and not Christian charity that
had driven them from their homes to the old
lime tree. But that does not prevent their
thoughts from dwelling constantly with the
bellringer in his belfry, and from anxiously
counting how many periods he will toll. Ah!
he has finished at the second ; it is a woman
then who has blessed life and died. If he
had tolled a third time, it would have been
a man.

New astonishment, new surmises under
the lime tree ! What woman can it possibly
be ?   From which part of the village ?

The gossips are determined to wait for
the bellringer at all costs, so that they can
cross-examine him as soon as he leaves the
church. Let the cattle meanwhile low at
the empty manger, the omelette frizzle to a

cinder, the cat get into the store-room and steal to her heart's content; let the husband grumble at the dinner being late—they will not budge while their curiosity remains unsatisfied. What does a little grumbling matter, when one can snatch news red-hot? The husband will soon forget his grievance when the wife comes out with her brand-new intelligence. Not only to-day, but for four days running the latest death will form the sole topic of conversation.

To whomsoever this may not be a repetition of a well-known feature, it should be known that gossip in and out of season is as indispensable to us mountain-dwellers, as water to a fish. If anyone ever were to stop our talking and chattering, he would condemn us to death. We who live around the Jeschken Mountain would rather do without daily bread and content ourselves with dry potatoes, than renounce our sweetest habit. We will never give up gossiping; it eases life's burdens, steels our courage, keeps us healthy—in short, gossip is as important as going to confession. No girl would go haymaking, no child pick strawberries, no man set out on a journey, no old woman gather dry sticks alone. Otherwise we should get bored, and all the work would be spoilt.

But when there is some one with whom we can chatter about possible and impossible things, dear me, how the task does fly ! How quickly we get on with it, so that the dwellers of the plains cannot take their eyes off us.

The gossips are on pins and needles, and can hardly wait for the bellringer. What an age the man is taking to-day before coming down, and limping out of the church door ! He is really getting too old. The priest ought to look out for a smarter man !

At last he appears on the threshold.

' Whom have we lost to-day, goody ? ' they cry in chorus, and with a noise that drowns even the rattling and screeching of the keys in the lock, which usually searches marrow and bones.

' What ? You don't mean to say you don't know ? ' asks the cunning bellringer, holding up his hands. He is still a jolly old soul, although his head is as white as an apple-tree in the spring; it is covered with snowy curls, and he is bent with the burden of years.

' How do I account for this ? There's something uncanny about it. You will see I am right when I say that the old prophecy will come true. If such an extraordinary thing happens as your not knowing what is going on, our mountain will disappear and a great lake come in its place.'

'Come, come, you've made enough noise from the belfry for us not to forget that you are the sacristan. What are you rattling on for now ? '

'How can I help being surprised ? So far you have always known everything that happened exactly an hour sooner than those whom it most concerned. I could not dream that you should not have known of Lukas's young wife having blessed this life, and gone to her rest in the Lord.'

'Lukas's young wife ? That can't be true ! That is impossible ! I met her last night in the lane.'

'I saw her hanging up her washing yesterday.'

'I've told you the truth. Lukas's young wife has blessed this life. She died a few minutes before noon, and left a little daughter.'

'Poor wee thing ! What a hard parting that must have been ! Poor wretched mother ! '

'They say she died an easy death; she did not know she was going where all of us who are standing here will have to go; one a little sooner, the other a little later. She went to sleep and did not wake up again.'

' God give her eternal rest.'

' And a happy resurrection. We can't say she had all the virtues, but she was not a wicked woman.'

' Lukas won't fret to death about it.'

' Rather not ! He only married her in obedience to his parents, who threatened him with their curse if he would not do as they wished.'

' Bah ! whoever saw her and Lukas together could not help thinking that those two should never have been married. Lukas holds his head high, and looks about him as though the whole world belonged to him ; but she went about with a drooping head like a sick bird. She had no life and no spirits in her, and she wasn't healthy.'

' Well, now Lukas can choose as he pleases. I'm glad for his sake. I couldn't help being sorry for him when I saw him going to his wedding past this lime tree ; he was as pale as if the bridesmaids had led him to his death and not to the altar. Every one will wish him happiness and content. There are not many like him. He hurts nobody and will allow no one to be wronged. Where he can do you

a good turn he does it with all his heart.
He has a temper, that's true, but who is
perfect ? '

'Who could have prophesied to Vendulka
Paloucky that she would marry Lukas after
all ?　Since the day when his banns were up,
she hasn't gone to a single dance or feast,
and yet Vendulka is a spirited girl, and nimble
as a doe.　Because she was not allowed to
marry Lukas, she would not be any one else's
wife.'

'But why were his parents against her ?
I can't take that in.　She is a good, handsome
girl ;　she is not poor either, and she's
thoroughly fond of work.'

'And she's a sort of cousin of his.'

'That is just why he was not allowed to
marry her.　His parents were of the old
confession, and believed they were committing
a sin if they let them marry, because their
great-grandfathers were brothers.　Even the
priest could not persuade them.　They thought
that no one but themselves understood the
will of God.　They really imagined they alone
of all people possessed the key of heaven.'

'So that was it ?　I've often and often
puzzled about it.　You see, I married into
this place only a year ago.　Vendulka's heart

will be beating, if she knows for whom they
were tolling.'

' Lukas won't wait long before he marries
again, and it wouldn't be sensible if he did.
The cowshed full of cattle, the house full of
servants, and a small child in the cradle—a
man cannot do long without a woman in the
house under those circumstances. When the
six wéeks of mourning are over, and the last
mass has been said for the deceased, he is
sure to go straight to old Paloucky's and ask
for her.'

*   *   *   *   *

They had not been mistaken. Everything
happened exactly as the gossips under the
lime tree had made out.

Six weeks after the death of his wife, on
the day on which the last mass had been said
for her soul, the widower and all his male
relations — according to the uses, or rather
abuses, of our country—went to the inn, to
drink off his sorrow. He remained there with
them till dinner time treated them to the usual
sumptuous meal. When this was finished,
he thanked them all for giving him their
company on this and on the day of the funeral,
and begged them for their further friendship.
They, of course, promised this readily with

many handshakes, and demanded on their
side that he should remain to them true as
friend and relative, and he also promised this
with lips and hand. Then there was general
embracing and drinking to each others'
health. At last Lukas rose and looked
towards his brother-in-law who was sitting
next to him. He too rose and, wishing his
guests the best of health and further amuse-
ment, the widower at once left the inn. No
one asked where they were in such a hurry to
go, but all smiled a friendly smile at him, and
winked knowingly at each other.

And what speering and looking there was
from behind all the windows when the two went
through the village together! Although no
one had the least doubt where they were
going, all wanted to see with their own eyes
whether they were really off to Paloucky's to
get his consent. When the neighbours saw
that they were actually turning in there, they
at once got ready to follow them. The custom
in our country demands that when a would-be
bridegroom and his groomsman are seen to
turn in at a certain door, the villagers should
follow in close upon their heels. As a rule
the people divide ; if the parties cannot at
once come to terms, or one of them demands

impossibilities, one half supports the bride-groom, the other the father-in-law.

The Palouckys' house was always kept spotlessly clean, for Vendulka was as particular as if she had been town-bred. But on this day more than usual care had been taken to clean and tidy everything, as though it were the eve of a festival. The floor of the room and passage had been amply strewn with white sand; the black frames round the pictures of saints had been pasted with leaf-gold and stuck with green boughs; the window-panes were polished so that each one should catch the rays of the sun at their brightest. And yet it was neither a saint's day, nor the eve of a festival. Clearly then, rare and honoured guests were being expected.

Lukas, although he had avoided meeting Vendulka during the six weeks of mourning, so as to give no offence, had probably given her a hint through a trustworthy person that he intended to call and ask for her father's consent. She must also have communicated this news to her father: otherwise old Paloucky, called "the Moper" behind his back, on ac-count of his extreme bigotry, and of his find-ing cause for dismal reflection in every event that happened, would hardly have put on his

Sunday clothes on that day, nor parted his long hair carefully and smoothed it down on both sides of his face ; nor provided himself with a freshly filled snuffbox. He welcomed the widower and his brother-in-law with beseeming civility, but did not fail to heave a deep sigh. He was perpetually brooding on the sins and follies of this irreligious world, and had become so melancholy about this that he looked quite wan. He offered his guests armchairs, and in a dismal tone asked them to take a rest. But they refused his offer with thanks.

'There will be time for that when we have learnt how you will receive our request,' said Lukas's brother-in-law, 'no doubt you know without our telling what we have come for.'

Old Paloucky sighed again ; he was always most unwilling to take a part in worldly affairs, but he could not help himself on this occasion and had to bite into the sour apple.

He was probably anxious to shorten the disagreeable task that lay before him as much as possible, so he showed at once that he had been instructed in this matter.

'It would be a lie to say that I was ignorant,' he said. 'I suppose Lukas wants to marry our Vendulka ? '

The brother-in-law could not suppress a smile at the Moper's unusual smartness; as a rule he took a long time before he said what he was going to say, and pondered long and thoroughly, so as not to endanger his salvation. It is to be regretted that people of this kind are dying out: formerly all our mountain dwellers were equally cautious and conscientious.

Lukas too was smiling contentedly to himself, pleased to hear Vendulka's name coupled with his own. He was only at that moment beginning to believe that all that had happened in the course of the last six weeks was true. He had lived through the weeks of mourning as in a dream, unable to realize this sudden turn of his fortune. He warmly replied : 'We two would have come to terms three years ago if my parents hadn't interfered, isn't that so, uncle ? '

'What d'you mean by that ? ' said the Moper in a depressed tone.

'What do I mean ? You would have been as glad to give me Vendulka as I should have been to have taken her.'

The old man again looked perplexed ; for some time he did not answer, then he slightly shrugged his shoulders.

Lukas, the rich peasant, good neighbour and well accredited man, had hardly been prepared for this answer.

'What is it you would have had against me, or what's wrong with me ? ' he cried, and the blood mounted to his face.

The old man was startled by his violence.

'Don't shout,' he calmed him timidly, 'do you not know that we sin against God Almighty when we give way to vain wrath and fury ? '

'Why then, tell me straight out why you would not have cared to give me your daughter. Did you consider me a spendthrift or a windbag ? Or did you think she wouldn't have had enough to eat in my house ? Perhaps you don't care to give her to me now ? '

'Oh yes, I am quite willing to give her to you. How should I not, since you hold her so dear ? '

'And is that the only reason ? '

'Let me alone with your questions if every answer makes you wild.'

'I shall ask what I want to know ! I want to know what's wrong with me, and why you don't give me your daughter as willingly as I should wish.'

The Moper pondered for a considerable

time; it was obvious that he did not quite know how to extricate himself.

At last he decided for a straight course, reflecting that that always leads you furthest, and besides it would not be seemly for him to prevaricate.

'Well then, if I as a Christian am to tell you God's truth then . . .'

'What then?'

'Then I tell you that as a father I would give you my daughter willingly, and do not know any one whom I would rather have as a son-in-law. But all the same I do not advise this marriage either for her sake or for yours.'

Old Paloucky wiped away the beads of perspiration that stood on his forehead. How importunate this fellow Lukas was! But perhaps it was as well that he had been so pressing, for it had given Paloucky an opportunity of saying what had been a load on his conscience ever since his daughter had told him of Lukas's intentions. Otherwise he might not have dared to come out with it. Now it was over. But it had cost him a good deal of perspiration.

Lukas and his brother-in-law were speechless with astonishment when they heard these words, and silence had also struck the

neighbours and gossips who, one after the
other, had crept into the room to be witnesses
of the betrothal. They would have expected
anything rather than such a development.
There had been but one opinion for years on
the whole mountainside that no two people
had ever been made for each other as Lukas
Paloucky and Vendulka Paloucky were. The
village had been full of the tale of their unhappy love affair, of the admirable faithfulness of the girl, the deep grief of her lover who
had been yoked to another woman. Every one
rejoiced and was glad for their sakes that they
should come together after all. Their marriage
was being looked forward to with the pleasantest
anticipation, as though it were a great festival.
And here was the Moper, saying incompre-
hensible things! But the villagers soon regained their usual balance of mind. They
looked at each other as much as to say:
'We know him; it is an old story that he
spoils every game.' Lukas, however, was not
satisfied, and repeatedly pressed the old man,
saying : ' If you do not advise the marriage,
you must have a reason. Do you think Vendulka cares less about me now ? '

'Don't talk nonsense. You know very
well that she has had eyes and heart only for

you. If your wife hadn't died she would have remained single to her dying day. She has had handsome and very acceptable offers from all sides, but if I had counselled her to accept one, she would not have listened to me in the least.'

'If one of them had dared to go past my house after he had been accepted, he would never have reached his home alive, I swear to you!' Lukas cried with such violence that the old man shrank back frightened to death and again entreating him not to sin against God's mercy. Lukas's face was aflame with passion, but that became him well, very well. He was a fine fellow, this Lukas; he had an air and ways as though the whole world belonged to him.

'Just as she never left off loving me, I have had her in my heart all the time,' thundered the young widower, without paying any attention to those exhortations. 'During the marriage service I could hear nothing but her sobbing in the organ loft. I was not far from leaving the bride and the priest at the altar and running up to her to take her to my heart, and no one would have torn me from her alive. It was not for the sake of the bride that I remained on the stool of repentance. I hated her because she insisted on marrying me when she knew I hated her, and insisted although I cared for another, and did not rest till she had got round my parents. I held out on account of the old people, so that they should not say shame had killed them sooner than God had meant to call them to Him.'

'Let wife and parents rest in peace,' his uncle timidly warned him, 'do not call their shades from the grave with your unnecessary talk, or they might come to my bedside and demand an answer from me why we have disturbed their peace. The dead to the dead, the living to the living! I have told you already that I have nothing against you; I know you for a good, law-abiding and obedient son, and a kind neighbour. If my words, tentatively said, are displeasing to you, you have only yourself to blame for having urged me to speak out. I said them to satisfy my conscience and to warn you, so that you should not blame me when you have come round to my opinion. But enough of this, we will now talk business. I shall give my daughter Vendulka a thousand florins. When you take her to the altar, I will pay you the money down on this table in silver currency. She shall also have an outfit such as becomes a bride. If that satisfies you, give me your hand.'

Old Paloucky held out his hand to Lukas.

The widower took it hesitatingly and said : ' I did not ask for any settlement, I don't care whether you give your daughter anything or not : I ask for nothing but the girl. If we two, after so much trouble, now come together, I shall envy no king. To be sure, far rather than have your thousand florins I wish you had not made that insinuating remark which has given me great pain. And do not think, my dear uncle, that I shall give you peace until you have told me quite plainly why my marriage with your only daughter is not as agreeable to you as I had hoped and thought.'

These words, said in a tone of real distress, did not fail to make a great impression on the future father-in-law.

' Well, my dear boy——' he hesitated, fearing a fresh outburst of wrath, and yet willing to grant a reasonable and civil request, ' do you want me to tell you what I really think ? I fear, there will be no blessing on your marriage.'

' No blessing ? Do you think in your heart as my parents did ? '

' Yes and no. I have no objection to your

being blood-relations, as our Church does not forbid such marriages. But I do dread your both being of the same temperament. Vendulka won't give in once she takes a thing into her head; she would sooner see the world in ashes. She has an iron will in everything, not only in love. And you, my dear boy, so far as I know, you are not an angel of patience either when you have set your heart on a thing. I fear that when your two hard heads knock against each other, you will see stars and not know where in the world you are; and then things will go badly, very badly indeed. —Now you know everything, you have got it all out of me to the last word; now leave me alone or else your wooing will put me under the earth. See how the sweat is running from my forehead. I want to have peace from you; your love affair has cost me trouble enough. For the short space of time that is left me, I want to have peace to prepare myself worthily for the grave time of reckoning and my meeting God. So I am telling you beforehand, don't come to me with your complaints. I don't want to have my life embittered any more by your affairs. If you should not get on together—I don't want to know anything about it, any more than you want to listen to me now. Don't come to me with your quarrels; my door will be closed against you. Now you know ! '

Old Paloucky had spoken the latter part of his admonition with so much emphasis, that the bystanders realized he meant it very seriously. It rarely happened that his great conscientiousness would allow him to commit himself to a definite statement. As a rule he gave the impression that on further reflection he might come to still better conclusions. But when he spoke like this, every neighbour knew only too well that nothing on earth would move him to a change of opinion.

He was mistaken in his fear of a fresh outburst of fury on the part of the bridegroom. Lukas only laughed heartily, and the others joined in his merriment. Every one thought that this was the Moper's usual way of hitting the nail on the head.

' If you like, uncle, I will give you a written statement that you are exempt from knowing either me or your daughter if we should fall out ever so little,' he proposed to his future father-in-law in the highest of spirits.

Nothing could have seemed more ridiculous to him than the idea that he could quarrel with Vendulka, with his Vendulka ! For her sake he had often raised the youth of the village in the night-time against the old man, to help throw large stones on his roof and disturb his sleep, for he could not forgive him for guarding his beautiful daughter with Argus eyes How could he quarrel with Vendulka, who had never been absent from his mind for a moment while he was married to another ; who had refused every suitor for his sake, although neither he nor she could have known that fate would still bring them together ?

Well, old Paloucky did not bear his nickname in vain, it fitted him exactly. Who would have thought that even the present occasion would give him cause for moping ?

The groomsman who was shaking with laughter, as well as every one else, went off to fetch the bride.

When Vendulka had seen the bridegroom entering the house, she had hidden herself, as a good old custom demanded of a well-brought-up girl, and had waited in her bedroom till the groomsman should call for her, to tell her the result of the preliminaries, and to lead her to the bridegroom, who would then repeat his suit to her.

Vendulka came into the room with the

groomsman. When Lukas saw her who shortly would be his bride he grew quite pale with excitement. 'Lukas,' she said, and held out her hand to him, while the tears poured from her eyes. Lukas greedily seized her hand and pressed it to his heart.

'Lukas, believe me or not; perhaps it would have been better if we had never found each other than at this price. Maybe the poor woman had to die because I never thought of her except with bitterness, and grudging her the place at your side. I can't get rid of the thought that my feeling like that may have hurt her, although father says it is a stupid idea, and God works His will without minding human wishes. But ever since I have learnt for whom the death knell was tolling, my tears have not ceased to flow.'

Lukas tried to comfort the weeping girl, but he himself had tears in his eyes.

Not indeed for his dead wife ; but he thought how long it was since he had held Vendulka's hand, and that he had had to pine through his best years without her, tied to a wife he did not love. Whoever saw these two young people standing together, holding each other's hands and looking at each other with moist eyes, must have borne the old Moper a grudge for his eternal whims and premonitions. Were they not made for each other ? Both were of tall stature, well grown, with the eyes of swift does, and beautiful jet-black hair curling at the nape of the neck. They were absolutely bound to fall in love with each other, whether they would or no ; that was clear to everyone present. And equally clearly they were bound to come together, in despite of all the powers of darkness, were they sworn against them. One might say their destiny was written on their foreheads, and that they belonged together.

' If you are so sorry for his dead wife, you will be all the kinder to her child,' the brother-in-law led off the conversation again, when he saw that Lukas was speechless with emotion. ' As you probably know, my wife has looked after his household so far. She has been very pleased to do it for him, but she can't go on. We have a large household ourselves and children like organ-pipes. If my wife has to go on running away at any moment, we shall come to grief ourselves. I should have said nothing if you could have been married in a week's time ; but as it is, because you are relations, you must wait for the Bishop's dispensation from Leitmeritz.

That will be a long business, maybe it will take two months. I therefore ask you in the name of all Lukas's relations, to take over the care of his household at once for love of him, so that he need not take a stranger into his house who would probably go off with what she could lay hands on, and perhaps neglect the child as well.'

During the groomsman's speech Vendulka had gradually calmed down.

'Why do you make so many words about it?' she replied. 'What sort of woman should I be if I left the care of my lover's household and his motherless child to a stranger? What would Lukas, what would you all think of me,' she continued in a re-proachful tone, 'if I made difficulties about helping him in his need? I don't know what I myself should think of a girl who refused a similar request! I think I should advise her lover not to marry her, as she could not pos-sibly have a spark of real devotion for him, and would be altogether without feeling. Of course I will take over Lukas's household, and will do so at once, so that your wife can stay at home with her work and her children.'

All the bystanders heartily approved Vendulka's warm words. It never occurred

to any one to think the groomsman's request
peculiar, or to take offence at the bride's
willing acceptance. On the contrary, they
would have been offended had she answered
differently, and severely blamed her for
letting a strange person take over the care
of her lover's household and child. The
usual custom in our mountains is for the
bride not to go to her husband's house till a
few weeks after the wedding, but only when
it is convenient; it is just as usual, when
circumstances demand it, for her to go to her
new home as soon as the banns are published.
She does so when her mother-in-law is very
old or bed-ridden, and wishes to be relieved
of the household cares; or when the daughter
who had done the work marries; or when
illness, demanding immediate and urgent care,
has broken out in the family. In short, as
soon as the bridegroom has got his father-in-
law's consent, the bride considers herself as
belonging more to his family than her own,
and feels it her duty to help him under all
circumstances, as befits a true and faithful
companion. The bridegroom, on his part, is
also ready to help her family as though he
were a son.

Everybody had predicted that Vendulka

288 B3

would go to Lukas's house immediately after
the betrothal, to put his bereaved and
neglected household in order. His first wife
had been known to be a bad housekeeper ;
then she had died so suddenly and everything
had been at sixes and sevens. Every one was
now looking forward to Vendulka's management of his affairs, and, taking all things into
consideration, thought the brother-in-law's request a natural and inevitable part of the
suit.

The most indifferent person among the
onlookers was the bride's father, who took no
notice of such trifling things. Let his daughter
and her lover do about them as they pleased.
He now looked upon her as belonging to
Lukas's family more than her own, and he was
thankful that she would soon be leaving his
house altogether. He was hoping confidently
for the return of those quiet days in which he
would be able to prepare himself at leisure
for his journey from the valley of tears to a
better land. Hitherto he had been disturbed
and hindered in this important duty by the
constant contemplation of his daughter's
misfortune ; her frequent and passionate outbursts of despair had embittered his mind.
In addition to this he had had to deal with

frequent offers of marriage from her numerous
suitors, who urged him, as her father, to
support their cause.

It was not without good reason that
Paloucky had reproached Lukas with having
caused him endless trouble and difficulties.

To pass the time agreeably to himself and
others during the preliminaries, he took much
snuff and frequently made the snuffbox
circulate. When Vendulka and Lukas at
last had come to an agreement, and sealed it
with the customary handshake, he sent for
beer from the inn and for new bread and goat's
cheese from the larder, so that it should not
be said his guests had had to leave his house
with a dry mouth after Vendulka's betrothal.
They did not wait to be pressed to eat, but
fell to, and drank each other's health in many
glasses.

Lukas was the only one who cared neither
for food nor drink. His eyes were continually
seeking his sweetheart, who had disappeared
from the moment when he had taken the
head of the table at his father-in-law's request. From that time forth she had not
been seen again. He did not want to ask
after her for fear of being laughed at. But
he missed her sadly, and did not enjoy the

feast. As soon as his brother-in-law with the advent of twilight began to get ready to leave, he jumped up from his seat and, without minding the others, went with great strides into the hall to look for his sweetheart.

He ran up against a maid-servant, and asked after her. She opened her eyes wide in astonishment. Thinking that she might be deaf, he repeated his question. At last he got an answer.

'She's been off ever so long ago.'

'Where to?' asked Lukas who was as astonished at her answer as she had been at his question.

'Where should she have gone?' the maid said, gaping, 'where in the world but to your house? When I went for the beer, she was packing up her things in her bedroom, and when I came back I saw her close to your house.'

Who would doubt but that Lukas did not want to be outdone by Vendulka in proof of steadfast devotion? Shouting as he bounded along the road, he ran home, and entered the room quite out of breath. He found his sweetheart by the cradle of his motherless infant. Again she was weeping bitterly, as before, when his brother-in-law had led her to her

bridegroom and the lovers' had looked into
each others' eyes again for the first time.

Lukas dared not break in upon her mood
with outbursts of his boundless happiness.
Content to know she was with him, he stood
by the window and waited for her to calm
down. The sun was just setting behind the
woods ; everything was bathed in gold. The
western sky, flushed with crimson, was glowing
like a sea of fire.

To Lukas all this seemed indescribably
beautiful and magnificent, and in his happiness
he fancied he was on the eve of a great festival
which would last for all the rest of his life.
How many times he had stood at this window
and looked at the evergreen woods, and thought
of Vendulka's faithful love which was as
lasting and true as the green of yonder pines.

On countless days the sun had set in such
glory as this, but to him it had seemed veiled
in gloom, like everything else in the world.
Nothing could please him ; life had held no
joy while he constantly had before him her
whom he disliked, and had to keep out of the
way of the one for whom his heart was pining.
How often he had stood at this window and
silently accused his parents of having brought
this hard fate upon him ; how often blamed

himself for having given way to their urgency,
when he knew that he would only bring un-
happiness upon himself with his marriage.

Gradually Vendulka seemed to regain her
composure, and slowly tore herself away from
the sleeping infant. Lukas also turned away
from the window and looked round. He then
noticed the exemplary order and cleanliness
of the room. Vendulka had tidied everything,
and washed the table after she had given the
servants their supper. The young housekeeper
had no sooner set foot in her future husband's
house than his household had become her
first concern. Again Lukas experienced a
feeling of great happiness when he saw that
he and Vendulka were at one also in this
respect. It had always been his special wish
that the servants should receive their due
punctually and in proper course. How often
had not his first wife's carelessness about this
annoyed him ! He could see in every detail
that henceforth a different spirit, a new life
would enter into his house. And the old
Moper would have him believe that their
temperaments were not suited to each other !
Just because they were at one in so many
respects, they would understand each other
all the better.

Lukas expected Vendulka to come to him; he hesitated to go to her, fearing he might upset her as she had been so excited. But Vendulka was making a close inspection of the spinning wheels and spindles near the stove, to see whether the maids were keeping them in proper order. So he approached her after a time and, sitting down on the stool near the stove, he looked at his handsome bride with all the intense love which his heart held for her. Again, as in the afternoon during the settlement he was speechless with emotion. She too was silent, and busied herself with the spinning wheels.

At last Lukas began with a voice choked with emotion: 'It is good of you to be so fond of me.'

She looked at him with astonishment, and if her heart had not been so sore at the thought of the dead woman and her innocent babe, she would have laughed aloud at his remark.

'Is that a new thing, that you praise me for it?'

'Well, it's not new; I only meant to say that we should never have found each other but for your faithfulness.'

'Yes, to be sure,' she assented, 'for us two things have come right. But your dead wife

has had to suffer for it. It is a sad thing that
one man's joy is another man's sorrow. But
I will make up to her child what she has done
for me in giving up her place at your side to
me. Just now, before you came into the
room, I promised her that I would sooner lose
my hand than touch a hair on her little girl's
head or let it be touched. She will see if I
keep my vow faithfully when she comes to
visit her. Not once shall she have to change
her linen, not once to make her bed. She
will always look as if she had grown out of
the water, poor little mite! I shall expect
her every night. I shall put ashes on the
floor round the cradle and look for her footprints; they say, spirits do leave footprints;
ever so light and feeble, hardly to be seen.
You have heard that, haven't you?'

Lukas nodded, but he hardly knew to what
he was assenting or what she was talking
about, although his eyes were fixed on her lips.
But he was not looking at them so as to catch
the sense of the words she was speaking.
His eyes sought them because they were so
charmingly red and cherry-ripe. Of course,
Vendulka was now ten times more beautiful
than she had been when he had roused the
whole village for love of her, and exasperated

the old man, for his daughter dared not come
out to meet her lover. He would have fetched
her in with a hazel switch if he had suspected
her of loitering outside the house. When she
bade him good-night, he had always laid it
down by his bedside with a significant look at
her, as she turned to go towards her bedroom.

No, it was impossible! Lukas could no
longer only look at these lips; he must feel
how warm and sweet they were.

And before Vendulka knew what he was
doing, he had jumped up, caught her in his
arms and pressed his mouth upon her red lips
so hard that he nearly drew blood.

In angry surprise Vendulka tore herself
from him and pushed him away with all her
strength. Lukas was not prepared for this;
caught unawares, he reeled back into the
room.—Every one knows how powerful our
mountain-girls are. They easily lift their
partners into the air at the 'longest night'
dance during the contest after supper.

'Aren't you ashamed of yourself?' she
rounded upon him, and flushed scarlet, as
though the evening sky had been reflected in
her face.

'Gracious, what a to-do about a kiss! As
though to-day had been the first time I had

taken one from you,' Lukas tried to conciliate her, while he did not seem disinclined
to repeat the offence.

' I don't say it is the first time, but previously
you were free. It was no one's concern if *I*
didn't mind. But now you still belong to
your dead wife.'

But Lukas would not hear of such a thing,
and strongly resented the inference. ' Oh no,
I have been mourning my wife as I should,
from her funeral to the last mass for her soul
this day. I haven't spoken of you once all
that time, nor looked at you till after I had
told old Martinka to let you know what
I was going to do. At mid-day I publicly
drowned my sorrow at the inn with my
friends, and all that is now over and done
with. Ask whom you will, they will all tell
you that I am as good as a bachelor.'

' I don't ask other people what I ought to do
or not to do, and no one need tell me, because
I always know my own mind. And I tell you
that I am not going to be made love to under
your roof where the feet of your dead wife
have barely grown cold. I don't care if the
whole world should prove to me that I am
in the wrong. There's time enough for that
sort of thing after the wedding when we two

really belong to each other, and she will have no right to mind.'

' It's true that you are ten times prettier now than three years ago when I used to rouse the whole village for your sake, but you were ten times nicer then. Just think how you used to shout with joy when I crept along the willows by the brook and into your garden at twilight, and you waited for me under the aspen. You flew into my arms with delight then. Why this coyness all of a sudden ? '

Although Vendulka gave him an arch smile when he reminded her of those evenings under the aspen, she turned a deaf ear to his reproaches, and would not grant a second kiss on any account whatever. Her anger became violent when he put his arm round her neck unawares. How could she have the heart to frown so severely, and to threaten him that he would be sorry for what she would do to him if he did not leave her in peace. But when he would not be put off, and kept on teasing her, she seized him, and before he knew what she was doing, she had put him out into the passage, bolted the door on him, and barricaded it with the table, to prevent his return to the room.

For a long while Lukas stood outside in the

dark as though he had fallen from the clouds.
This was not as he had pictured the evening
to himself when he had sped home after
Vendulka on wings of love. But he mastered
the feelings that were rising in his heart, and
tried to smile at what had just happened as
at a jest that had missed fire. Who should
have a right to jest if not a bride with her
future husband? It is her prerogative to
tease and annoy him a little.

So Lukas walked away from the door of
his room without trying to enforce an entry.
With the happiest of faces he mixed with the
servants, pretending that he had come out of
his own accord so as not to be in her way.
He listened smilingly to their praises of the
new housekeeper, and to their congratulations
of him and themselves on such an excellent
mistress. And when it was time to go to
sleep, he crept into the hayloft with the men,
where he had been in the habit of spending
the night since the death of his wife.

*　　　*　　　*　　　*　　　*

He turned restlessly on his couch, wondering why Vendulka had been so prudish with
him and, although her eyes had betrayed
passionate love, had been cold and reserved
in word and deed. What was in her mind?

Was she afraid that now that she was his, he would hold her less dear, as men sometimes do? That therefore it was prudent to be more reserved and to put him off? How could she so misjudge him? It was just because of her sincerity and undisguised surrender that he valued her so highly, and he had been happy to know that there was nothing but truth behind every one of her glances and words. At last he resolved not to trouble his head about it, and not to try to know the reason for this sudden change in her. Perhaps she hardly knew herself. Women sometimes took an obstinate notion into their heads, and when you asked them the reason for it, they could not tell.

It was of no consequence. What did a kiss matter? If not to-day, she would give it him another day. The chief thing was that he had her with him on his farm, by his fireside, with his child, and no one had a right to interfere or take her from him.

' She will change her mind to-morrow, she won't be able to keep it up longer,' Lukas repeated to himself, and to comfort himself he recalled those lovely evenings under the aspen tree.

Firmly convinced that those hours of bliss

would return, he at last put worrying thoughts from him, and shut his eyes for sleep when the cocks crew for the third time behind the shed, reminding the maid-servants that the sun had risen from his bed of roses and the new day demanded its share of work.

But Lukas made a mistake when he confidently expected Vendulka to change with the next day. She was exactly the same on the second day, and the third did not differ from the second. She stood firm on her ground that no caresses and kisses must pass between them before their marriage, that to do so would mean troubling the rest of the poor woman in her grave, who had to quit this world so that they might be happy. How else could they conciliate her? What could they do for love of her otherwise than show by their restraint that they valued her memory and held her in high esteem?

Lukas could get nothing out of Vendulka by love. Her sophistries and reasoning displeased him, and she would listen to nothing that he said against her point of view. He could not find it in his heart to treat her roughly. So he resorted to entreaties. He no longer demanded the kiss as a proof of her love, but of her compliance.

' You are not a little child, Lukas,' she said
reprovingly, ' a man ought to have more in-
sight, not less than a woman ; why are you
so slow of understanding in this ? It almost
annoys me that you should be.'

Lukas had failed again in spite of all he
had said, reasoned and urged. At last the
thought occurred to him that his sweetheart
was perhaps purposely tormenting him, because
it gave her pleasure to think that he was head
over ears in love with her.

Perhaps she was enjoying the sight of his
passionate unrest ? How could she have
failed to notice that he thought her ten times
more attractive now than three years ago, and
that the sudden sight of her, or the sound of
her voice when he heard it unexpectedly,
made him start ? With her quick perception
she would no doubt be well aware of this ;
but was it kind of her to torment him out
of mere wanton pleasure ? Perhaps to laugh
in her heart about his love, and think : ' I
can do with you as I like, you won't escape
me ! ' Some people only value what is
unattainable. When it is within their reach
it has no further attraction for them. Perhaps
she was one of these ?

Gradually Vendulka's attitude roused him

to resentment, and after a week he frankly
told her that she did not seem to him as
kind-hearted as he had thought three years
ago.

But Vendulka pretended that she had not
understood him, or that his words had gone
in by one ear and out by the other; she
never gave him a definite answer. She was
otherwise kind to him, looked so happy and
ran about with an expression of so much
delight in all her duties, that no one could
fail to see she was in the seventh heaven.
Whoever looked into her beaming face, felt
the happier for it. Lukas also was glad of
it; he too seemed to be in heaven when she
smiled her happy smile at him, and looked
at him with her lovely expression. But as
soon as he sat down beside her to talk of love's
sweet delights, she would remember some work
that needed doing, and before he could prevent
her, she had torn herself away and was gone.

During the short time since Vendulka had
taken charge of his household, everything had
taken on a different look. Every part, to the
remotest corners, was spotlessly clean and
tidy; it was a pleasure to look at it. From
early morning till late at night Vendulka was
cheerfully doing her work, trying to make up

with her industry for the carelessness of the woman who had died. She really had not much time for talking. But what did Lukas, being deeply in love, care for all her work, her clever management of the household and the change she had worked? He wanted his kiss; the rest she might as well have left undone.

Who will blame him when he lost patience with her in the end, as he could do nothing with her either by love or by threats? He at last became really bitter against her and unable to master himself any longer; he angrily stamped his foot one day.

'Listen, Vendulka, let's make an end one way or another, I am sick of this to-do,' he cried, hoisting the storm-signals. 'If you do not immediately embrace me as you used to do under the aspen tree, you will see me do something that you won't like. I shall go to the inn this minute, and not come back till the sun rises on yonder mountain.'

The blood mounted to her cheeks; it was easy to see that his threat frightened her, but she would never have dreamt of giving in.

'If you haven't learnt sense at your time of life, go and welcome!' she answered abruptly, and ran off.

That was more than Lukas had bargained
for. He had thought that, if for no other
reason, she would have given in for the sake
of appearances. Now that he found he was
disappointed, he had to make good his boastful
threat. So he took his cap and went to the
inn which had never had any attraction for
him, and now less than ever. While his wife
was alive he had only occasionally gone there
when he felt too miserable in her company,
and his longing for Vendulka had been over-
strong. He left his house with gall in his
blood. Now he would take his revenge of
his prudish and heartless sweetheart! When
he returned from the inn at a late hour, he
purposely upset all the pails and milkcans
in the hall, so that she should hear the noise
and think that he had come home drunk—
because of her.

How could Vendulka have failed to know
that all this nonsense was happening on her
account ? She had meant to be really angry
with him, but when he chose to make a noise
as if Beelzebub himself had taken possession
of the place, she nearly died of laughing. He
meant to punish her, and was only punishing
himself ! She knew quite well that he did
not care for drink, and equally well that,

unless a man is inclined that way, he does not
become a drunkard in one night.

When she saw her lover again in the
morning she did not mention what had
happened the night before. She spent as
little time as possible with him, and hurried
off to her work. She was afraid of laughing
in his face, if their conversation were to
last long. The trick he had played upon her
would not have surprised her if he had been
a boy of sixteen. But she had not expected
it of him, such a discreet man and greatly
esteemed, and a widower into the bargain!
Fancy upsetting pails and milkcans on account
of a kiss! Her manner irritated Lukas more
and more.

'If she is going to play the obstinate, she
shall feel that I am a stiff-necked one too,' he
decided, and, without saying a word about
it at night, or saying good-bye to her, he ran
off to the inn directly after his supper, as if
it had been a settled thing between them
that he would go there if and when he liked.
But on the next morning also Vendulka remained as dumb as a fish on the matter. No
—things couldn't go on like this! She must
have exemplary punishment for her obduracy.

'Every one was singing your praises last

night,' Lukas began smilingly; 'because I now sit at the inn till break of day when I never used to formerly.'

'They must be wise people who blame one person for another's follies.'

'They know quite well that I should not seek their company if you behaved as you should.'

Vendulka felt this was beyond a joke.

'What am I neglecting in my duties that you talk to me like this, and try to make people gossip about me?'

'The first duty in every household—the master.'

Vendulka became pensive. How was it possible that Lukas should misunderstand her intentions which must be as clear as day-light to every one? Only a person evilly disposed towards her could put her in the wrong about it. Or had her father been right after all with his doubts and his warning?

'I know you are sensible and kind-hearted,' she said at last, 'why do you now dissemble, and pretend you are neither? I have told you more than once that it was not for the sake of love-making that I came to your house: there will be time enough for that.

I have come because there ought to be a mistress on the farm, and your child needs a mother. My idea was that your brother-in-law had asked me to come for no other purpose than that. If I had dreamt that you had had other intentions, I would never have set foot in your house.'

'There you are! You admit that everything in the house matters more to you than my happiness. And do you imagine that does not give me pain? Is that the way to thank me for being so faithful to you all these years? For your sake I never once looked kindly at my wife and was always grieving to see her in your place. But I must say one thing for her, whatever else I had against her: she would sooner have bitten off her tongue than denied me anything; my will was hers. I should not blame you if I had asked anything impossible from you. But now I am asking for nothing but a single kiss, to let me see you care for my wishes. And it is not the kiss either that you mind; you are only denying it to show you don't care for me. Do you think that does not annoy me? If I asked any girl of my acquaintance, she would give me a kiss for friendship's sake, willingly and without prudishness.'

' But I am not " any girl." '

' You're right there. Any other would have given heart for heart, it's only you who gives pride for love.'

' If you think love means no more than two people kissing each other, you do not know what love means, and never have known it. I don't care for such love.'

' And I don't care for love without kindness and gentleness.' Saying these words sadly and impressively, Lukas went out of the room, thinking more than ever of the Moper's words. What he had said was unfortunately only too true ; he was a wise and experienced man ; only a fool could have disregarded his warning.

This time Vendulka was sorry to see Lukas turn away from her. So far he had only been annoyed and angry, but now he seemed seriously offended, perhaps he really doubted her affection, as he could see nothing but obstinacy in her attitude. That he could take this view had grieved her unspeakably ; she minded it more than the comparison in her disfavour with his first wife. She was startled, and not without reason, to think how far things had already gone between them, that such words could have been spoken.

These melancholy reflections brought the tears to her eyes. She thought long and seriously about Lukas and about herself.

'After all, would it matter,' she pondered, leaning her perplexed head on the hood of the cradle, 'if I gave him his heart's desire, to-morrow morning before he goes to work?' She pulled herself up with : ' Enough of this,' but continued to reason in the same strain. ' It might not offend the dead woman, and yet show him that I can do something for him even if it goes against the grain. But no—no, I will not do it! I am not standing out for appearances but for my deepest convictions and in an honourable cause. What would have happened if his wife had never yielded her place to me, and everything had remained as it was ? We should have had to make the best of it. No, I will stick to what I have decided upon; I know I am doing right.'

Her father had had good reason for saying that his daughter had an inflexible will, and would not yield even if her world should be consumed in fire and flame. Of that which she thought right Vendulka would not yield a hair's breadth.

When from that day Lukas never lost his sad expression; when he never sat down at her side, and spoke no more than was necessary; when he went out every evening, staying away till daybreak, it dawned on her that with all her good intentions she had taken the wrong turning. She realized that it was wicked to drive him further on his downward path, that she must save him from ruining himself. He might in the end make a habit of things to which he had at first only turned from vexation and ill temper.

'Don't forget that you have a child, Lukas,' she at last warned him, when she saw him take another florin from the drawer, after he had put one in his pocket the night before only.

'You do as you like, and so do I.'

'We should always listen to well-meant advice.'

'I never once listened to advice my wife gave me who was fond of me, and would not think of following yours, who are not.'

'What in the name of Heaven do you mean? I—you say—I not fond of you? Who was it told me in this very place three weeks ago how unspeakably happy he was in being certain of my affection?'

'I did not know you then as I know you now. I should have expected death rather than your driving me from home and enjoying what you are doing.'

Vendulka found no words to reply to these unjust reproaches. She felt she would lower herself in arguing with him. She suppressed the bitter feelings that were rising in her heart, and turned away in silence, but he only saw another proof of her pride in this. He decided to revenge himself by another visit to the inn, and stayed away even longer than usual.

Vendulka spent the night in great excitement, and prayed to God to illumine the Bishop, so that he should make haste and send them the dispensation. These continual bickerings and quarrels filled her with great apprehension for the future. How differently she had pictured to herself the life at his side ! How they had longed for each other ; how many tears they had shed for each other, looked forward to the moment of reunion—and now ? Now everything went wrong, and for absolutely no reason. But this was just why Vendulka would not give in, nor Lukas either, who became more embittered and unmanageable every day.

Sometimes they both felt their heads reel at the thought of what was to be the end of

it! Nevertheless, neither of them gave way.
He demanded that she should recognize his
right to her personally for the sake of his love,
while she expected him to appreciate her
straight and honest character and her steadfastness. Meanwhile the breach between them
gaped larger and larger before their eyes, and
they began at last to look at and speak to
each other as enemies. Alas! Why were
their temperaments so similar? Even the
Moper had probably not guessed how soon
their happiness would change.

At last Vendulka's long repressed sorrow
found vent in tears. In the same room and
on the same seat near the stove, where the
disastrous quarrel had begun, she broke down
and wept bitterly. Her tears flowed un-
checked, and she took counsel with herself
what she should do when Lukas returned
home from his work in the evening.

When he came in, she had not yet made
up her mind. It startled him to see her
weeping so bitterly in his house, and the last
occasion on which he had seen her cry like
this occurred to him. It had been on the
last evening which they had spent under the
aspen tree together; when they had both
thought that they were taking leave of each

other for ever. He too took counsel with himself, whether it would not be better to give in, and not demand the kiss until after their wedding. A man should have more sense than a woman. Why embitter each other's lives ? They were really fond of each other, had thought to die because they had not been allowed to marry, and now, shortly before their wedding, here they were, tormenting each other for no reason whatever.

'Why are you crying ? ' Lukas asked his sweetheart in a gentle tone, such as she had not heard from him for a long time.

'I hear you have now taken to gambling at the inn as well ? '

'I have learnt many things lately that I knew nothing of before.'

'But above all you have learnt to do things to annoy me.'

'What about you ? '

'I am behaving in your house as a decent girl should. I think I deserve praise rather than blame for that.'

'You think I ought to praise you into the bargain, because you jeer at me for dancing to your piping ? Tell any one how you are treating me, they wouldn't believe you. Show me a bridegroom who has had to put

up with so much annoyance from his bride
shortly before the banns are published. But
mind! I'll let you know that I am not a
silly boy in his teens who can be led by the
nose. I won't be treated like this! I shall
do to you after the wedding as you have done
to me now when you have hardened your
heart against me. I have quite made up my
mind on that point. Wait and you will see
me do it.'

It was foolish of Vendulka to turn pale at
these words. She might well have known
that he was only a man in a temper, and it
would have been better if she had simply
said: 'Don't talk nonsense!' Possibly all
would have been well. A woman who cannot
lead a man with gentleness when he is storming
and shouting with anger, will never manage
him at all.

But these heartless words had barely
escaped Lukas, when Vendulka behaved as
if she had lost her senses.

'It is not written in any book that we two
must be married,' she cried in a voice trembling
with anger. 'If that is how you feel about
it, and you are preparing nothing but shame
for me, I should do best to leave your house
before I kill myself with misery.'

Now it was Lukas's turn to become as pale as a corpse.

' You're not making many words about that,' he shouted, ' but try it, and see what a welcome you will have from your father ! And don't imagine that you will have suitors by the dozen. They all will see that you are not what you pretended to be, else you would not leave your bridegroom when you had come to his house to take care of him.'

' You know better than any one else whether I have ever minded what men thought of me. I don't care for any of them, and I don't care for you either. I've had to do without you once, and I shall do so again.'

Lukas ran out into the open like a wounded boar ; he felt as though poisoned arrows had pierced his heart. What could he do to her to make her feel the same burning resentment that her barbed words had caused him to feel ?

Vendulka had done wrong in answering him so uncompromisingly ; but he did no better when he revenged himself on her by taking home a brass band from the inn and making them play one piece after another under her windows. The band, however, was the least offence. Why should they not have played to him if it amused him, and he made it well

worth their while ? But he brought with
him three girls who did not enjoy the best
reputation, else they would not have gone
with him, when they knew that he was be-
trothed to another. He then proceeded to
dance with the girls so furiously that the
house shook.

Crowds of spectators arrived on the scene
to enjoy this exhibition. They all laughed
at the bridegroom's mad behaviour, and made
conjectures as to the causes of this disgusting
spectacle. Vendulka could hear every word
through the open windows. She dared not
shut them for fear of drawing the people's
attention upon her. What she heard made
her feel sick. No! she would do wrong to
put up with this scandal ; it had evidently
been Lukas's intention to hold her up to
public ridicule for having pined after him for
years.

When he had at last taken himself off with
his crew, when the screams and laughter died
down in the distance, and darkness fell,
Vendulka hastily gathered up her belongings
into a bundle and took leave of the sleeping
child. She bent over the cradle to which
she had come on that first night with many
good intentions in her warm heart, and burst

into a flood of tears : ' I must leave you, because I held your mother's memory in high honour,' she whispered, kissing her, ' tell her that, when she comes to see you. I wanted to make up to her for the happiness she gave up when she made room for me. Happiness indeed ! I am now running away from him to whom I was so eager to come. I hope that whoever will come in my place to take care of you will be as good to you as I have been. But poor, poor thing, if it is one of those he is now caressing ! '

Then Vendulka roused one of the best and most faithful maid-servants from her sleep, gave her all the keys of the house and made her responsible for the child, about whom she gave her the most minute instructions.

' Where are you going so late in the night, and why do you talk as if you were leaving us ? ' the maid asked in astonishment and alarm.

' I am going away for ever,' Vendulka answered sadly. ' I am going to the town to look for a place.'

Before the maid, who was speechless with fright, could regain her composure, Vendulka was gone. She had run off hastily, so the weeping girl had not even heard her footfalls,

and could not tell in which direction she had
gone.

* * * * *

Old Martinka got up from her bed and
lighted a candle. She started; it was nearly
eleven o'clock. She ought to have been on
her way through the forest by this time.
But her rheumatism had kept her awake,
and so she had ended by oversleeping herself.
She would willingly have given a silver threepenny if she could have lain a little longer and
slept to her heart's content, but there was no
help for it; she was expected, and must
needs creep out of her feather-bed. What
would old Matouš say if she did not come to
fetch the contraband?

He had hinted at silks which would have
to be hidden in the bushes and under trees,
as it was impossible to convey them to their
destination at once, and he could not do this
without her help. The customs officers and
the police of the whole neighbourhood knew
him for a bad penny, and had their eyes on
him. Even with his cleverest moves he
would not have succeeded in getting through.
—Ah! things did not come as easily to her
as they used to. Her old legs were longing
for rest and comfort. Martinka was right

to think of the lean years, and she had
made her little pile. She had no need now
to be afraid of old age and illness. If she
had found a dependable assistant whom she
could have trusted, she would have sent her
in an emergency like this ; she might even
have thought of retiring altogether. She
herself had never cared about a life of comfort.
But where were such people to be found nowadays ? Did any of the young women want
to work really hard ? Weren't they all afraid
of danger, as if they were made of glass, and
of the rain, as if they were made of sugar ?
Wherever she went she secretly made inquiries for a strong, discreet girl or a widow,
who would not be afraid of serving the good
cause by day or night, storm or frost, wind
or snow. But she had been unsuccessful so
far. Vendulka only recently had refused the
offer with a shrug of her shoulders, when
Martinka had told her of the hope she had
cherished with regard to her services. Vendulka
had said it was a precarious thing to join
the smugglers ; not only good health was
needed but a particular kind of recklessness
which hardly one girl in a hundred would
possess. Since that day Martinka had almost
given up hope of realising her wish. When

Vendulka had made a decision, it was once and for all.

Martinka was the sister of Vendulka's mother, after whose death the child had come to her for comfort, and remained with her for several years. Vendulka did not care to live at home, partly from grief for her mother, partly because she did not like living with her father, who forbade all loud and cheerful noises in his presence. She therefore was almost one of the family, and Martinka talked over her affairs with her as with her own daughters; these would even reproach their mother with caring more for her than for them.

Lukas knew well how dear old Martinka held her little Vendulka, and that their affection was mutual. He therefore had chosen her to announce him as her suitor, knowing that his offer would be all the more graciously received if it came through her.

Vendulka was right in saying that hardly one in a hundred women had the necessary gifts for the smuggling trade.

Martinka herself had only gradually acquired her skill, and it had taken a long time before she got accustomed to turn day into night, and to creep along lonely passes and byways in the dark, endure the hardships of winter, and

be for ever on the look-out. It was always on
the cards that one of the frontier-police might
be hidden by the wayside and suddenly spring
upon her, inspect her basket, and if she did not
pay the duty, take her off to the magistrate.

But she had not had much choice at the
time. When a man dies and leaves his wife
an empty cottage and five hungry children,
a woman cannot be too particular. She must
take what comes along and be glad of profits,
however small. How should she have refused
from mere niceness what was very profitable,
and certainly not bad or dishonest ?

Old Martinka saw nothing wrong in her
trade, and all the people in our mountains
share her view. Nowadays the trade has
lost much of its profit and is a poor one,
but thirty or more years ago it was a
very different matter ; a nice little fortune
could be made by it, and it was not only a
poor beggar or tramp in the last ditch who
took to it, but many of the better class who
looked upon it as a means of adding to their
income. They considered smuggling a trade
like any other, with only this difference that
it was forbidden officially. Martinka had
been acquainted with the smugglers even
before her husband's death, as he had

frequently concealed them in his cottage,
which was conveniently situated for their pur-
poses, being at about half an hour's distance
from the village, and quite hidden by bushes.
The place was called 'the firs.' No one
could see who was passing in or out of it,
unless he stood close to the fence.

When her husband died the smugglers had
asked Martinka to join them, out of gratitude
for his many services to them. They expected
her to meet them regularly at night in some
lonely spot in the forests which cover the
frontiers of Saxony and our mountains. She
then had to take over part of the contraband
and carry it to the next place of appointment,
whence it was taken by other trustworthy
persons to its ultimate destination, which
would sometimes be as far off as Prague.
Martinka had gratefully accepted the offer.
She had now distinguished herself by her
skill for many years; had made a living for
herself and her children, helped them to
obtain good situations, and saved a nice little
sum for herself. What other trade would
have done as much for her? The 'blackies'
employed several women carriers, but none
of them worked to their satisfaction as
Martinka did. Her 'Capo,' old Matouš, who

with his five sons did a roaring trade by
smuggling, had often been heard to say that
he would give up the whole business if ever
Martinka gave it up: the other women
caused him too much trouble and annoyance.
You never could tell what they might be
up to. One had lost part of the goods en-
trusted to her; another had not hidden them
skilfully enough and so spoilt them; a third
suddenly and without any cause had taken
alarm and thrown away her basket. They
did more damage than they were worth. How
should Matouš not have been annoyed with
them? He often lost patience with them,
and patience was such a necessary attribute of
his trade. After all, when he came to think of
it, there was now no great necessity to put
up with them. ·He had made his pile, and
what he now did was more from habit and
as a pastime. He was a widower, his sons
were married. What was there at home to
amuse him? He preferred to roam.

Old Martinka was a past-master in dressing
her basket. When one of the police met her
in the mornings in the woods, it did not occur
to him that her basket could contain anything
besides the eggs or apples which she had
heaped up on the top, or to ask her any

questions. She showed them such an honest
face, said good-morning so simply, and told
her beads by the way with so much devotion,
that no one would have taken her for anything
but an honest egg- or apple-woman who had
got up early, and was now hurrying to the
town by short cuts to steal a march on the
other market women.

If in spite of her precautions one of the men
stood still and looked at her with suspicion,
she at once stood still too and offered her
produce. Who could have doubted her
sincerity? It had even happened that the
police had bought pears or cherries from her
without finding her out. What wonder that
old Matouš appreciated her, and praised
her to the skies, saying that such women
were not born in these latter days, and
that she would be the last to tell of the old
glories.

Still grumbling with annoyance at having
overslept herself, old Martinka hurriedly
wrapped herself in a warm shawl, took her
basket and once more overhauled its double
bottom and the shoulder straps. Then she
wedged in two pieces of wood crossways about
a hand's breadth from the rim, covered them
with a board on which she laid several pounds

of fresh butter, and spread a cloth over the top.

When she was just on the point of starting, some one came running full tilt towards the door of the cottage. Martinka stopped short; she thought this might mean a police raid. But by the dim light of the rush-candle she recognized—Vendulka Paloucky.

At this hour of the night Martinka would sooner have expected to see a ghost than her niece, and at the first moment she was speechless with astonishment and apprehension. Without bidding her aunt good-even, Vendulka dropped on to a seat near the door, and groaned as if she were in agonies.

' Thank God a thousand times that you had not yet started,' she stammered at last.

' But for the Lord's sake, what are you here for at this hour of night ? ' asked Martinka, when she had regained her composure; ' your face is on fire, and you have no breath left. I suppose Lukas's baby is ill, and you want me to get you medicine from Zittau through the smugglers. Be quick and out with it ! I'm in a hurry, I ought to have been on my way by now. I don't know what Matouš will think ; he will say I am no better than the other women.'

'There is no medicine in the whole world for the illness that has driven me from Lukas's house,' said Vendulka, and hot tears were gushing from her eyes.

'What? What is that you are saying?'

'That my engagement to Lukas is broken off, and we shall never meet again.'

'Girl, you are out of your senses.'

'I will soon prove to you that I still have my senses, although enough has happened to make me lose them. Lukas made love to me the same as he used to do when he was free. I wouldn't let him, out of respect to his dead wife, whose rest in her grave I ought not to disturb. Then he behaved as if he were demented, raved and scolded, and constantly found fault with me, so that I grew hot and cold to think what would be the end of it. And this night he brought a brass band to play under our windows, and three loose girls, and he danced with them in front of the house to make me the butt of shame and ridicule. After that I could do nothing but pack up my things, and here I am. I dare not go home; you know that father told me beforehand, Lukas and I were not suited to each other. His sermons and his reproaches for not having listened to him would be the death of me.

I don't wish to go into service in the town either. I should die with home-sickness among strangers, and with longing for our mountains and our speech. Then in my trouble it occurred to me that you were in need of an assistant. You won't find one who is more devoted to you than I am, and you will soon teach me the rest. You know that I am not timid or spoilt, and I am not stupid either; I would rather be with you than anywhere else. The neighbours know that you are either asleep or on the roads, so they don't come to see you. Nobody will know that I am with you, and if you ask the smugglers not to tell, none of them will gossip. Lukas will think I have gone into service, and leave me in peace. I need not fear to be bothered either by him or by father; neither of them will trouble about me, they will be glad to be rid of me.'

She could not go on, her face betrayed her despair.

'What frights you give people, you young devil!' Martinka scolded her niece. 'I really thought something dreadful had happened.'

'What? Is that nothing? Didn't I tell you how Lukas has put me to shame before the whole village, and why?'

But Martinka only shook her head, annoyed

with Vendulka for having startled her so unnecessarily.

'What Lukas has done, any other man in his place would have done,' she said disapprovingly to the sobbing Vendulka. 'What bridegroom would like his bride to set a person who is dead and gone above him, even if it should be his own wife? I can't understand why this didn't occur to you before you ran away. He is not the first man to be made mad by such behaviour as yours. Have you forgotten our Mráček, who went to keep house for her lover in a similar case? He too was a widower and had two children. She was just like you, and would not let him think of frivolous things; she was afraid of the dead woman's ghost coming to her bedside at night. And what did he do? Slit up all the feather-beds and emptied them into the street—a regular snowfall we had, although it was St. Peter and St. Paul's. And don't you remember Kavka? When the bride forbade her bridegroom to pinch her cheeks, so as not to offend his wife in paradise, did he not straightway go to the grocer's, bought up all the beer and emptied the barrels down the gutter, simply to annoy her? My dear girl, men are men; they want to be the masters at

any price. You won't change them, nor I.
When a bride goes to keep house for her
lover before the wedding, she lets herself in
for much trouble, but in return her husband
will love and honour her to the end of their
days. You can't have something for nothing,
honour is dearly bought. The only thing
about it that annoys me is that your father
should have proved to be in the right. Fancy
you letting it come to that! Why couldn't
you let Lukas rave and fume? Why retort?
It serves you right that you should have had
a taste at once of what obstinacy and bad
temper lead to. In the future you will be
careful not to go too far. But your anger
doesn't impress me at all. It is like thunder
in the spring, short and furious; everything
is the more beautiful and luscious for it afterwards. You will make no one believe that
you can live without Lukas or he without
you. You make me laugh. You two will
attract each other for ever; as long as
you live on this earth you won't get rid of
each other. When Lukas comes to his senses
he will be annoyed with himself for the trick
he had played on you; and if you will sit
here and think about it till to-morrow morning,
all sorts of things will occur to you which you

ought or ought not to have said.　Your wrath
will go up in smoke when your blood has cooled.
You will be reasonable, and the old love will
come back all the more strongly.'

'Never—never!' Vendulka cried with all her
might.　She had hardly been able to contain
herself to the end of her aunt's admonition.
'I don't deny that I loved Lukas more than
my life, but now—now I hate him like death.
Oh God!　What a dreadful thing to say!　I
cannot think how I can bear the pain of saying
it.　He was not like this formerly; his dead
wife has spoilt him.　Yes, it is her fault, she
has spoilt him for me.　He says himself that
he could do as he liked to her.　She didn't
mind what he did.　That is bad for a man.
A girl like me needn't put up with everything.
She was careless, and didn't do a thing well,
but I am a first-rate worker in the house and
on the farm.　Every farthing I take for milk
and butter is booked, and I can read every
book in the old spelling or in the new.　And
I demand nothing but what is right and
fair!　You think I shall change my mind by
sitting here and thinking things over till to-
morrow morning?　You mean to say you are
going off and leaving me here alone?　For
Heaven's sake, don't do such a thing, I should

get desperate by myself. Think of my
misfortune ! The man for whose sake I have
scorned all the others, who was the first in
my heart after God Almighty Himself, has
held me up to ridicule before all the world,
and threatened to make me miserable after
we were married. My hair stands on end
when I think of it. Aunt, you must take me
with you to make me forget my sorrow ; if
you leave me here, I shall die.'

Aunt Martinka had not the heart to refuse
this pathetic appeal.

'Well, it doesn't matter for once, and you
won't want to come a second time—gently,
gently, don't be up in arms again, I suppose I
may still say what I think ? I will bet you
anything that we shall not even finish a loaf of
bread together in this house. Come in God's
name ! Take that basket and strap it on
your back. I shall take it easy by your side,
to make up for the fright you gave me. But
you mustn't walk upright like that ; bend
down low, so that every one can see you are
carrying a heavy load. You know yourself
what a basket of that size weighs when it is
full of butter. You mustn't look as if it were
full of feathers. If you want to go in for
smuggling, you must pay attention to these

things; sometimes the smallest detail will become a pitfall. That's right! Now let us be off under God's protection, and mind you start with the right foot forward, so that we may both come back safe and sound. You needn't be afraid of my smugglers, they do not look like dandies, but they are very respectable people, especially old Matouš. Do you know him? He never misses going to Church on Sundays and Saints' days, and always stands close to the pulpit, to hear God's word first-hand. Church and sermons, that's what he likes, he is very devout. He never smuggles during Lent, and he doesn't smoke, so as to make Providence look in favour upon him. In short, he is a very good man, just like my poor husband; they might have been brothers, those two. He is still as smart at the trade as his youngest son, no one can beat him at it. He is the leader of the party, and has ten or twenty followers. They walk one after the other at a distance of a hundred steps; they glide like shadows. Formerly there would be as many as fifty, but like everything else, the trade is going down. He climbs the rocks like a chamois and has the hearing of a partridge; he smells the police half a mile off. As soon as he

notices the slightest thing wrong by the way,
he makes a sign to the others and leads them
on byways and paths where spies daren't go.
I am now meeting them in the woods of Kries-
dorf, near the "bonny well." Matouš himself
usually meets me there with his bundle; he
doesn't get on with the other women.'

They had stolen out of the house during this
conversation and taken to the woods. Then
they walked along in silence.

Vendulka felt the cold, deep, damp darkness
of the woods enfolding her, and heard the eerie
rustling, sighing and groaning overhead, without knowing whence these strange, mysterious
sounds came. Were they really produced by
firs and larches, or was there something
else sorrowing between heaven and earth?
Cold shudders were running down her spine.
Sometimes she felt as though she were walking
at the bottom of a deep lake, and the waters
were moaning over her head. She thought of
a fairy tale which a tenant in her father's
house used to tell her on the seat by the stove,
on winter nights:

' There was once a town which was suddenly
engulfed, and a lake appeared in its place—
and all this happened because the town had
harboured a traitor. It is said that to this day

bells can be heard on the shore of that lake, which the inhabitants down below are ringing for help.'

Did this tale occur to her now, because she herself was on the brink of ruin, and because she was harbouring in her heart love for a man who had been a traitor to her ? Was that why her heart was beating so sadly, like the bells of the engulfed town? Fear and a horror hitherto unknown took possession of her ; she had never been in the forests at midnight. Accustomed to houses surrounded by fields and gardens, she was not used to its mystery.

' And yet I would a thousand times rather be in the forest alone at midnight, a thousand times rather serve the smugglers as a common carrier, than lower myself to be the footstool of an unjust man who persecutes and scorns a woman because she is steadfast,' she repeated to herself over and over again, and then her fear and horror would yield to bitter resentment. Yet it was impossible now that she was alone in the world, and sadly wandering through the darkness, not to remember the joyful, happy day when she had flown on wings of love from her father's house to that of her bridegroom to become an unspeakably happy, honoured, loved and loving bride. On that

day the western sky had been glowing like a
sea of fire; her eyes had seen the heavens
open, and her heart had been full of the
presentiment of a great happiness. But none
of these dreams of bliss and love had come
true; all the hopes of her young life had been
blighted. How should her heart not break
with the pity of it all?

'I shall get over it, indeed I shall,' she
told herself, but a voice deep down told her
she never would, and that she never could
detach her heart from the man to whom it had
been so wholly given.

'I shan't tear my hair about it! Perhaps
he is now laughing at me with one of my rivals.
I won't think of him—I won't, he isn't worth
it! If I stay where I am, no one will tell me
of his new courtship and his marriage; no
one will praise his bride to me—her beauty,
his fondness for her. Fond? Could he really
be fond of her? I can hardly believe it. I
blame him severely, but to love another in
his place—no, even spite could not make me
do it! But men have quite different ideas of
love from ours; unfortunately I have had to
learn that. He was not like this before his
marriage, though! His wife has spoilt his
character.'

Vendulka was interrupted in her tearful soliloquy. Her aunt had stopped short, and Vendulka, who was following on her heels, was obliged to stand still also. The old woman drew a whistle from her knapsack and put it to her mouth; it gave a sound so soft that every one would have taken it for a bird piping his gentle midnight call in the top of a tree. Long-drawn echoes answered from the distance. Her aunt was delighted.

'Old Matouš is still on the watch,' she whispered, 'he knew I should come, even if it rained stones. He can depend on me. But now we must be quick and not keep him waiting longer.'

The old woman quickened her pace so that it was all Vendulka could do to keep pace with her. They reached a steep piece of rock, thickly wooded; Vendulka thought they would skirt it, but Martinka began to climb, holding herself upright; her niece scrambled after her. A sudden turn brought them to an opening in the rock, from which the shadowy form of a man appeared. It was old Matouš, who had been lying down in the grass, waiting for the arrival of his laggard carrier; he was now raising himself.

When he had heard a noise in the bushes,

he had taken a roll of material from under his coat, but as soon as he heard that two persons were approaching, he dropped the roll and put his hand in his breast pocket. Vendulka started and drew back; she saw the mouth of a pistol which was pointed at her head. However, the fright was all that she received. Who knows what might have happened if Martinka had not quickly stepped forward and explained who her companion was? But Vendulka had had a taste of what might happen to her at any moment, and she was trembling in every limb. The old smuggler laughed at her for her fear; a palm hard as bone was held out to her. But she herself did not feel like laughing. She trembled as if she had looked death itself in the face. Timidly she laid her hand in his, and thereby evoked a fresh burst of laughter.

Her aunt, he said, was made of different stuff, but of course such women were not born nowadays.

Meanwhile Martinka had hidden the roll of stuff in her basket, which she dressed again so that no one would have guessed it contained anything else than butter. But she would not allow Vendulka to carry it; she might have done something foolish, seeing that the mere sight of a pistol frightened her out of her wits.

Old Matouš nodded approval, and repeated that if Martinka gave up, he too would retire from business and not care what became of it. He told her she need not take the contraband farther than her home; a linen-draper from Reichenau would send for it, and deliver it to the customer who wanted the silks for her daughter's trousseau.

Old Matouš had hardly said this, when he disappeared suddenly, as if the rock on which he stood had swallowed him. Vendulka again shook from head to foot; his unexpected disappearance, his rough speech and uncouth gestures and his wild laughter had quite unnerved her. Oh Lukas, Lukas! What had he made of her! This was her reward for the confidence with which she had meant to lay the destiny of her whole life in his hands, and would not believe that happiness could come through any other man! Who could have thought that he would make her so unhappy? And she had been near to losing her life through his fault as well! Would he have been touched by the news of her death? Would he have come to the funeral? Would she have forgiven him in

her last hour ?   No—she could not have done
it.   But ought she to have taken her anger
against him into eternity, and complained
about him to the Almighty, when she knew
the fault was not really his, but his first wife's,
who had spoilt his character ?

Vendulka was trembling with cold and with
the mental agony through which she was
passing; and added to this was the fear that
perhaps the worst was still to come, and a
horde of police and watchmen would suddenly
fall upon her and drag her off to prison.

'Well, how do you like smuggling ? ' her
aunt asked with a sly smile, when they emerged
from the woods and turned towards 'the
firs.'

'Very much,' Vendulka hastily assured her
with chattering teeth.

*   *   *   *   *

Lukas with his dancers returned to the inn
at the head of the band, and whoever had good
lungs and sound legs in the village accompanied
him, to make merry at his expense, and dance
to their heart's content.

He had made up his mind to mete out
exemplary punishment to Vendulka that night
by making a general feast for his comrades
and all the merry girls who were no prudes.

and knew his true value. He gave orders to
the landlord to consider every one his guest
who came to the inn that night, and to fill
their glasses as often as they liked.

He danced merrily, with a full bumper in
his hand ; he had no sooner let go one of the
girls when he held the second in his arms ;
he need not call them, they came of their own
accord ; they vied with each other for his
preference. Each wanted to be first ; each
one had words of honey on her lips and fiery
glances in her eyes ; they would have
embraced him readily. Not one was afraid
of troubling his dead wife's rest ; he would
not have asked for their kisses in vain ; he
could have had as many as he wished. But
why did they not tempt him ? Why was he
so soon tired of it all ? Why did he leave the
dance to sit down by a table in a corner of the
bar, determined not to dance another step ?
Why did he look as black as if he were at
war with the whole world, pushing aside his
glass as though it contained wormwood ?
Why did he suddenly jump up to fly from the
inn as if some one had whispered in his ear
that his house was on fire ?

Lukas fled from the inn, from the music
and his partners, because a loathing of every-

thing there had come over him. In the wild noise and turmoil, in the midst of girls who cringed to him to win his favour and oust Vendulka from his heart, the reaction had set in. When the general mirth had risen to its height, when the women were prepared to go to any length to please him and draw him into their coils, Vendulka's image pursued him, and would not be banished. He could not help comparing her to those who were throwing their favour at him, and felt that with all her pride and temper, her masterful and sarcastic words, she was animated by a very different spirit. How passionately devoted she had been to him, yet how much restraint she had shown during all those years! How true and sincere had been her intentions, and how single-minded the proofs of her love for him! What she had given to him, she would have given to no other man; of that he was firmly convinced. But of his flatterers of to-night he knew that if he did not let himself be caught, the same words and pressures of the hand would be given to another eligible man to-morrow.

He had turned to these girls to annoy his sweetheart, and they themselves had made him realize, what he unwillingly had to admit, that Vendulka with all her faults was immeasurably above them in sincerity and purity of character.

In the stillness of the night he walked to and fro for a long while, trying to make up his mind to his future behaviour towards Vendulka. She had deeply wounded him with her harsh refusal ; she deserved that he should be cross with her for a long time after their marriage. Should he now go on meeting obstinacy with obstinacy, and breaking down her pride, to show that he meant to be the master now and for the rest of their lives ?   Would she have been sufficiently annoyed with what he had done to her this night ?   What would she˙ say when they met again ?   It never occurred to him that she could possibly have carried out her threat.

Our good Lukas was so deep in thought that he imagined himself still walking from end to end of the field at the back of the inn ; but he had unconsciously drawn nearer to his own farm.   He did not realize this until he stood close to the fence of his little garden.   Suddenly he heard a joyful cry, and a woman ran out of the house towards him.   It was the maid-servant.

'Oh, it's only you ? ' she said ın

a disappointed tone, when she recognized him.

'Well, and who else should it be ? '

' I thought the mistress might have come back with you.'

Lukas started ; he began to suspect that something was wrong.

' The mistress,' he faltered, ' where should she come back from ? '

Instead of answering, the girl burst into tears.

'What has happened ? ' Lukas urged in great agitation, ' why are you standing here at this time of night ? Why are you not in bed ? What are you crying for ? '

' How can I help crying ? ' sobbed the girl, ' when our mistress has left us for ever ? We shall never get one like her. You might go to the ends of the world to look for a better. We all of us loved her for her kind heart and her order and cleanliness. She thought of every one rather than herself, and was always ready to do you a good turn ; she never was proud. And what a good mother she has been to the child ; she will never get one like her. The little mite knew her quite well, and smiled at her when she gave her her bottle. Poor little thing ! She took in that she cared

for her and loved her as tenderly as any mother.
Now she is orphaned, and so are we.'

Lukas reeled and had to hold on to the fence.

' Then the mistress is gone ? ' he repeated
dully several times. He could not believe
that what he had heard was the truth.

' Of course she is gone ! How should she
not have gone ? ' the girl reproached him
bitterly. ' Any girl would have gone after
you had danced under her window with three
women. Oh, why must you go and raise a
scandal like that ? We knew quite well that
what she did was not bad. We have got our
eyes and ears too, and cannot help noticing
things. Such a thoroughly good girl, and
now shortly before her wedding she has to go
among strangers, perhaps even to Germany !
Yes, I am sure she must have gone into
Germany. Where else could she have gone ?
She had to leave the country ; in our country
people would laugh her to scorn.'

It was said of Lukas that he had no other
fault than his bad temper ; apart from that
he was the kindest, mildest, and most
benevolent of men, who would not hurt a
creature. He now showed that people had
judged him fairly. He not only took the
reproaches of his own servant quite meekly,

but he felt his heart warm during her tearful homily, as though he were waking from a heavy dream that had held him in its toils. The simple statement of Vendulka's goodness by this disinterested observer did more than any arguments on the right or the wrong of his case could have done.

Without knowing how he got there, Lukas found himself in his room and at the window where he had so often stood in the days of his married life and thought of his sweetheart. And he had stood in blissful silence at this same window and waited, on the evening when his heart's desire had come into his house for the first time.

He had looked at the sky flushed with the crimson sunset, and fancied his life at her side would be one perpetual rosy dream. How different it all had been ! He saw his sweetheart flying from him in the dark, silent night, into a distant place, to eat the bitter bread of servitude with tears. It was in vain that he turned away from the window to change his thoughts. He determined that he would not let himself be carried away by the emotions that welled up in him, would not let them influence his reasoning, nor would he listen to the voice in his heart which clamoured for his bride. But wherever he turned his eyes, they fell on the traces of her activity. How charmingly arranged and cosy was his room ; she had an eye for these things, and no detail escaped her devoted attention. Yes, he might well go to the ends of the earth to find one like her ! His eyes fell on the cradle over which he had so often seen her bend—the sight of it stung him to the quick, and his sorrow mastered him completely. Why was it that she had gone ? What had driven her away ? It was that she had valued the memory of his own child's mother more than he had done.

'And if she were a thousand times in the wrong . . .' he at last cried so impulsively that the servant who was silently weeping where she sat by the cradle, jumped up in alarm.

'Hasn't she deserved that I should be indulgent with her ? I have been blaming her for her obstinacy, but when she refused one suitor after another, although she had not the least hope of our ever being married, I was glad enough of her obstinacy. It pleased me mightily, and I called it steadfastness, and praised her for it more than for anything else. What other girl would have forgiven me for

marrying another? Indeed, when she saw how
unrelenting my parents were, she herself urged
me to give way, and would not let them curse
me on her account. Any other girl would
have blamed me for giving ear to them more
than to her. From the beginning she has
been as good as gold, and cared more for my
honour than my love—and this is her reward!
I have tortured her for the sake of a mere kiss.
It is my fault that every one will laugh at
her, my fault that she is shut out from her
father and home, and has to go and earn her
living among strangers—but no, no, I shall
not let things go so far. I shall go to the old
man to-morrow and tell him everything. He
must find his daughter and let her know that
I will give her back her word if she hates me
so much that she wishes for it. But it shall
be in all honour, and as friends. I should kill
any one who dared to jeer at her; I'll let them
know! But where is the old man to look for
her?'

Lukas thought about this for a long time,
and consulted with the servant, asking her in
which direction Vendulka had gone; but
they could come to no conclusions. At last
it occurred to him that old Martinka would
be the most likely person to find her traces.

The old woman was always on the roads, and often heard the latest news. She could easily ascertain through the smugglers whether Vendulka had gone into Germany. For the moment Lukas suppressed every other feeling but the anxiety for Vendulka's safe return to her father and her usual surroundings with all speed.

He knew that old Martinka returned regularly before sunrise from her nightly raids. Dawn was approaching, and he started without delay to find her on her return.

He arrived at 'the firs,' but deep silence reigned at the homestead. He looked through the windows; the room was empty. The carrier then was still abroad. But she would not be long, for she did not like to be seen by day with her load in the woods. She surely must be back in a few minutes; the sky was flushed with red, and the sun was just about to rise over the ridge of the mountains.

Lukas leant against the fence and waited.

There she was, he could see her among the trees; that was her woollen shawl. But she was not alone, another woman was with her, probably an assistant.

He was just on the point of hiding behind the firs, to wait for the departure of the un-

welcome third person, when Vendulka's aunt
saw him.

' Lukas, Lukas ! ' she shouted madly to her
companion, who walked with her head bent.

The next moment the widower heard a cry
of irrepressible delight ; Martinka's companion
flew past the old woman ; two trembling hands
embraced him, and a kiss, a hundred times
more fervent than he had ever received under
the aspen tree, was pressed on his lips. Lukas
seized his bride by her belt, lifted her up and,
speechless with emotion, carried her back to
his own house.

*   *   *   *   *

What are we to think of Vendulka ? First
she stands out against the kiss, and rather risks
a scandal in the village than give it to the
lover with whom quite shortly she is about
to go to the altar—runs away, goes among
the smugglers rather than comply, and, after
the bitterest outbursts of wrath, gives him the
kiss of her own accord, unasked. Oh women,
women ! Which of them has not known her
heart run away with her reason when she was
least prepared for it ? God knows why this
is so. I have racked my brains about it in
vain, and yet it would be a good thing if the
matter were properly sifted once and for all.

But what is a reasonable being to say of Lukas, who boasted on his wedding-day to everybody that his bride ran away and joined the smugglers rather than grant him a single kiss before their wedding ? You should have seen how proud he was of this, how he praised her and showed her off with delight.

Can you guess who banged away the loudest at the wedding when the usual shots were fired ? Vendulka had many groomsmen, six riding alongside of her, and the seventh was best man. But more gunpowder than was used by any of these young fellows was turned into smoke by old Matouš. He held a pistol in each hand and fired two shots at the same time. When the other guests passed him, he stood still and banged away so that the gossips under the lime tree were wellnigh deafened.

Martinka, who was his companion, only smiled when he occasionally pointed his pistol at her head for fun. When Vendulka had asked him through Martinka to join the wedding-procession for the sake of the old friendship, he had asked himself why he shouldn't have a wedding of his own as well ? And he decided to leave the business with its daily toil and burden to his sons, and made

an offer to Martinka to do as he was going to
do, and give her old bones the rest they had
deserved. She might enjoy the few years
left to them in health and content at his side.
If they got married, she would not be dull in
her little cottage, and they could while away
the rest of their lives retired from business
and in happy talk.

Martinka consented and made ready for
the wedding at once. Now their banns were
to be published, and this was why old Matouš
made so much noise, and when Martinka
offered the loving-cup of rosoglio to the
gossips under the lime tree, none of them
was allowed to take a draught only; it had
to be emptied to the last drop. Not one of
the bridesmaids was so generous with her
gift—nay, the gossips never remembered
anything like it, though they had been
witnesses of many wedding-processions. Old
Martinka had spent a good margin of her
little reserve on this, but she was held in high
esteem for her generosity. For a long time
afterwards it was the chief topic of the neighbourhood, how splendidly she had celebrated
the wedding of her niece, Vendulka Paloucky.

THE VAMPIRE

BY

JAN NERUDA

THE unpretentious steamer which plies daily between Constantinople and the Princes Islands landed us at Prinkipo, and we went ashore. There were only a few passengers, we two and a Polish family, father, mother, and the daughter with her fiancé. But no . . . there was some one else. A young fellow, a Greek, had joined the boat at Stamboul on the wooden bridge across the Golden Horn. We concluded, from the sketch-book which he was carrying, that he was an artist. He had long black curls down to his shoulders; his face was pale, and his dark eyes deeply set. At first I was interested in him; he was very obliging, and able to give a good deal of information about the country we were travelling in. But he talked too much, and after ten minutes I left him alone.

The Polish family, on the contrary, was very attractive. The old people were kindly and gave themselves no airs, the fiancé was young and distinguished-looking, a man of the world. They were going to spend the summer at Prinkipo; the daughter was delicate and needed the air of the South. The beautiful, pale girl looked as if she had just recovered from or just fallen a prey to a severe illness. She leant on her fiancé's arm, frequently stood still to catch her breath, and now and then a dry cough interrupted her whispered conversation. Whenever she coughed, her companion stopped and looked at her sympathetically, and when she returned his look, her eyes seemed to say: 'It is nothing. . . . I am quite happy.'

They believed in her recovery and their happiness.

The Greek, who had parted from us at the landing-stage, had recommended an hotel belonging to a Frenchman, and the family decided to take rooms there. The situation was not too high, the view exquisite, and the hotel offered every European comfort.

We lunched together, and when the midday heat had passed off a little, we all slowly walked up the slope to reach a pinewood and enjoy the view. We had no sooner found a suitable spot to rest in, when the Greek reappeared. He only bowed to us, looked round for a convenient place and sat down at a few steps' distance from us, opened his sketch-book and began to draw.

'I believe he is sitting with his back to the rock so that we should not see his drawing,' I said.

'We don't want to,' said the young Pole, 'we have plenty of other things to look at.'

After a while he added,: 'I believe he is using us as a foreground. . . . I don't mind.'

Indeed, we had enough to look at. I do not think there can be a lovelier or happier place in the world than Prinkipo. Irene, the political martyr, a contemporary of Charlemagne, lived in exile here for a month. If I could have spent a month in this place, I should have felt enriched in memories for the rest of my life. Even the one day is unforgettable. The air was so pure and soft and clear that the eye soared as on downy wings from distance to distance. On the right the brown rocks of Asia rose from the sea, on the left, in the distance, were the blue, steep shores of Europe ; near us Chalki, one of the nine islands of the Princes Archipelago, lay mute and eerie, with sombre cypress groves ; it looked like a haunting dream. A huge building crowns the summit of the isle . . . it is a lunatic asylum.

The surface of the Sea of Marmora was covered with ripples, and played in all colours like a giant opal. In the distance it looked white as milk, near us it had a rosy shimmer, and between the two islands it glowed like a golden orange ; the depth below was sapphire blue. Its loveliness was untroubled, no large ships were moving on it ; only close to the shore two small boats, carrying the British flag, were cruising to and fro, a steam launch, about the size of a signalman's box, and a boat rowed by sailors ; liquid silver seemed to drip from their oars when they lifted them rhythmically. Fearless dolphins tumbled about close to the craft, or leapt in long semicircles across the water. From time to time huge eagles sailed from continent to continent in noiseless flight.

The slope below our seat was covered with roses in full bloom, the air was saturated with their scent. Sounds of music, vague and dreamy, rose to us from the arcades of the café on the shore.

We were all deeply affected ; our conversation stopped, and we gave ourselves up entirely to the emotions called forth by the contemplation of this Paradise. The young Polish girl was lying on the grass with her

head resting on her fiancé's breast. The
delicate oval face took on a faint flush of
colour, and suddenly tears welled forth from
her blue eyes. Her fiancé understood her
emotion, bent down and kissed them away,
one by one. The mother saw it and wept
like her daughter, and I . . . looking at the
girl, I also felt as though my heart was too
full.

'Here body and soul must recover,'
whispered the girl, ' what a wonderful spot ! '

' God knows, I have no enemies,' said her
father, ' but if I had, and met them here, I
should forgive them.'

His voice was trembling.

Again there was silence ; we all felt an
unspeakably sweet emotion. Every one was
conscious of a world of happiness within him
which he longed to share with all the world.
As we all understood what the others felt,
none of us talked.

We had hardly noticed that the Greek
had closed his sketch-book after about an
hour's work, and taken himself off with a
slight acknowledgment of our presence. We
remained.

When several hours had passed, and the
sky had begun to take on the purple tint

which makes the South so attractive, the mother reminded us that it was time to go in. We descended in the direction of the hotel, slowly but with buoyant steps, like children free from care.

We sat down in an open veranda in front of the hotel. We had no sooner settled down when we heard sounds of quarrelling and abuse below us. Our Greek seemed to have an altercation with the landlord, and we listened to amuse ourselves. The conversation did not last long.

' If it weren't that I had to consider other guests . . .' said the landlord, while he came up the veranda steps.

' Pray,' said the young Pole, when he came near to our table, ' who is that gentleman? what is his name ? '

' Oh, God knows what the fellow may call himself,' said the landlord bad-temperedly, and looking daggers over the balustrade, 'we call him the Vampire.'

' An artist, I suppose ? '

' Nice sort of an artist . . . paints nothing but corpses. No sooner has any one died hereabouts or in Constantinople, when the fellow is ready with his death mask, the very same day. That's because he draws in advance . . . but the devil knows, he never makes a mistake, the vulture!'

The old Polish lady gave a shriek; her daughter had dropped into her arms in a dead faint, looking like death itself.

Her fiancé leapt down the steps at one bound, seized the Greek with one hand and his sketch-book with the other.

We ran down after him; both men were rolling in the dust.

The sketch-book flew open, the leaves were scattered, and we saw on one of them a striking portrait of the young girl. Her eyes were closed; a myrtle-wreath encircled her forehead.

CHILDLESS

BY

IGNÁT HERRMANN

IVAN HRON had been married for ten years;
he had a beautiful wife and was rich. Even
his most intimate friends said, not without a
touch of envy, that he had ' a first-rate berth.'
They might indeed envy him, for Ivan Hron
seemed a spoilt child of fortune. When he
had left school, he had entered the university
to study law, in order to take his degree.
This he did chiefly because his father, a well-
to-do tradesman in the country, wished it;
he wanted his son to rise in the world. And
the son did as his father wished and went to
college. But he did not finish his university
career. As a young hothead he had been
mixed up in some political propaganda; the
affair had at first earned him several weeks'
arrest, then he was sent down. Although
his indiscretion had been of a purely political
character, the academic senate wished to
keep the reputation of the university unstained,
and parted for good with the ill-advised youth.

This outcome of his folly had so roused his father's anger that he ordered him out of the house and disinherited him. These things will happen ! For whom does a father work and worry from morning till night, if not for his children ? What right had a foolish boy, dependent on his father, to spoil his whole future by one careless act ?

That Ivan Hron had spoilt his, was his father's firm conviction, and he succeeded in convincing his mother too. With this conviction old Hron died.

And Ivan ? When he was in these desperate straits, he knocked at the doors of a Great Bank where clerks were wanted. He obtained work, and dedicated his mind and body to the concern for the salary of thirty florins. It was not long before his superiors found out that he had not wasted his time at the public school where he had spent the greater part of his life, nor during the two years at the university when studying law. Evidently he had after all not entirely spoilt his future outlook. His immediate superiors recommended him to the higher authorities as an eminently ' useful ' young man, and Ivan Hron got preferment. But his humbler colleagues had no idea of the surprise which

was in store for them when after a few years
the general manager died. While the cashiers,
head clerks, accountants, and other employees,
formerly of a very superior rank to Hron's,
remained at their desks or marble counters,
Ivan, who had assisted very successfully in
some important transactions, was unexpectedly called in at the board meeting,
where the chairman proceeded to deliver an
impressive address, full of oratorical flourishes
which befitted the occasion, and asked him
whether he would be willing to accept the
vacant post.

' We have the greatest confidence in you,'
he concluded.

Although Ivan Hron was exceedingly astonished, he showed his surprise in no way.
Up to a certain point he had confidence in his
own ability, and presence of mind enough to
answer that his acceptance would depend on
their conditions.

' The conditions will be the same that held
good for your predecessor,' said the chairman
of the board meeting, ' and if you fulfil our
expectations they will be better still. The
state of our affairs entitles us to great hopes ;
we only need a firm, energetic director. That
is why we have chosen you.'

Ivan Hron accepted, and the evening papers carried the news that same day to all those who were interested in the appointment of the general manager.

'Lucky fellow!' some said. 'They'll have a good head on their shoulders,' said others.

A most promising future now lay before Ivan Hron. He remained unmarried for another year, as though to test the ground under his feet. And when he found it was firm, he got married.

Many people were surprised that he had chosen a wife without a fortune. They were still more surprised when they heard that she had been an heiress until lately, when with the failure of her father's business the glamour which surrounded her had suddenly been eclipsed. Why had he knocked at that door when his position made him worth thousands? Was he under an obligation to her? Had he wooed her earlier and was now going to redeem his promises as a man of honour should? When circumstances take such a turn as his had done, surely promises are no longer binding, and so-called honour in these cases was ridiculous, said the more experienced and worldly among his friends and acquaintances.

Nobody knew that this unpromising match had cost Ivan Hron a great deal of trouble and perseverance; that he looked upon the father's failure as a happy coincidence; that the girl had yielded to the urgent request of her parents to accept the hand which was offering her a safe future, and which might perhaps save the whole family from the greatest misery. And Ivan Hron had beamed with happiness although he had led his pale bride to the altar and out of the church in an almost fainting condition.

He had now been married ten years. He was a handsome man in the forties, and some of his former fellow-students, now elderly clerks in lawyers' offices, unbriefed barristers, or doctors who had failed in their final examinations, looked with envy on the former student who had not finished his university career because he had been sent down.

Many of them were married and had several children; their wives had aged before their time, and often there was hardly enough for the current household expenses. Ivan Hron meanwhile belonged to the ' élite.' He had his carriage, was rarely seen on foot; his wife was still a beautiful woman, his salary increased from year to year; he lived in his own handsome villa, travelled for six weeks in the year, and had no children.

No children! His friends did not know how painful this part of his good fortune was to Hron. For none of the successes and attainments of his life gave him the happiness which a wicker-basket with muslin curtains and the downy head of a rosy, beloved small creature asleep in it would have given him. In spite of all the glamour of his brilliant, exciting life, Hron did not get rid of the old-fashioned feeling that life is perfect only when it is blessed with children. What point, what aim was there in his whole successful career? Why had he worked himself up to the highest position which was open to him, why did he save, to whom would he leave his fortune when, old and frail, he would end his days? What would rejoice his heart in old age?

Moreover, in his case his disappointment was not one of the accidents of life; he did not count how many years he had been married to his beloved Magda and still they were alone. He had married on purpose to have a family, and therefore this unfulfilled desire hurt him all the more. He had been bred in the country and was untouched by

the town-bred egoism which aims solely at
enjoyment for its own sake, at an untroubled
existence dedicated to the ' Ego ' and its
wishes. He wanted children, and when he
took his beloved bride home he looked forward
to holding a little creature in his arms in
course of time. Perhaps the full measure of
his longing for a family was due to his having
early been disowned by his own people on
account of his youthful folly; he had never
been received again under the paternal roof.
He longed to fill up this void by his marriage
to Magdalena. He watched her looks, almost
spied upon her sighs at night, and trembled
with impatience for the moment when she
would blushingly confide to him her sweetest
secret. But this moment never came. She
confided nothing; she went to and fro in
their beautifully furnished home, and her face
more and more distinctly took on a sad, almost
pained expression; a line appeared which
started from her prettily shaped nose and
included her lips. This expression did not
even quite vanish when she laughed heartily;
and when she was not smiling, the wistful,
sorrowful look quite gained the upper hand.

Was she too feeling what it was that made
them miss being perfectly happy ? Did she

know what was passing in her husband's soul? How could she have failed to feel and to guess? No one is so absolutely the slave of his will at every moment, that not a word or a look should betray what is slumbering in the depth of his heart, or what it is for which he is hungering and thirsting. Ivan Hron was no exception to the rule. There was hardly a moment when Mrs Hron did not guess her husband's wishes, if guessing indeed were necessary. Was she not a woman?

Hron would often invite friends to dinner or supper so as to have life in his empty, quiet rooms, and to see them a little untidy. There were times when he did not feel happy in the spotless surroundings of his home, where for months together everything stood in its appointed place, polished, and shining with neatness; where not a speck of dust was to be found, and the well-swept carpets hushed every footstep; where sounds of romping were never heard.

'You are living like a prince,' said one of his guests; 'how comfortable this house is, and how charmingly furnished.'

'And what lovely works of art,' added his visitor's wife, who did not get tired of looking again and again at the beautiful pictures and

graceful statuettes, or of turning over the
leaves of albums filled with photographs of
towns and lovely places which Hron either
alone or with his wife had visited. She looked
at the antique furniture almost with a touch
of envy.

'You do know how to arrange things,' she
sighed ; ' you are lucky.'

Ivan Hron looked round at the things which
had excited her envy, and looked almost
bored. They had interested him chiefly at
the time when he had bought them ; it gave
him pleasure to arrange them or put them up
on the walls, but after that he got accustomed
to them, seeing them every day, and in the
end he hardly noticed them. He said without
a note of pleasure in his voice, and thinking
of the rotund figure of the little woman :

' The rooms are pretty enough, but they are
too quiet. I wish there were more of us.'

He glanced furtively at his wife who had
ceased to smile ; he even thought that it was
all that Magdalena could do to suppress the
tears which were rising to her eyes.

Another time they themselves were on a
visit to friends who had three small children ;
the youngest was a charming, curly boy.
They were entertaining them with singing,

music, and animated conversation, but none of these things seemed to interest Hron. He devoted himself entirely to the little rascal in his high chair; he took him on his knee, allowed him to pull his nose and beard, chased him again and again under the table and caught him up to begin afresh.

Mrs Hron kept up the appearance of conversation with her hosts, but she was casting perpetual side-glances at her husband's game with the boy, and her eyes betrayed the pain which was wringing her heart. This one gift to him was denied her! How happy she would be if the laughter of children were to echo through their own house, if Ivan could chase a barefooted little fellow of his own!

In the middle of the game Hron suddenly lifted his head and caught one of these glances; he understood what was passing in her mind and left the boy alone. His absorption in the strange child must look like a reproach, and he did not reproach her, he loved her far too much for that. Had they a right, moreover, to reproach each other? Did any one in the world know whose fault it was that they had remained alone? Once he had taken refuge from his secret disappointment in a visit to a doctor, and confided in him. Was there a

remedy ? What could be done ? Whose
fault was this misfortune ? No, not fault, he
corrected himself; there was no fault, no
failing . . . but the cause, the cause ?

That was difficult to say. Sometimes it
was the husband, sometimes the wife—a
physiological problem, inexplicable. Perhaps
incompatibility, two natures which do not
meet; there was no explanation, no help.

Then Ivan Hron began to brood. He
thought over his past life; he was healthy,
without a blemish or taint. He must be
unsuitably mated then ? Perhaps he had
been too hasty about the whole affair.

How many times had he seen his wife before
their marriage ? Two or three times; first
in Dresden on a holiday. He had noticed a
gentleman and a charming girl who were
talking to each other in Czech. He concluded
that they must be his countrymen, probably
also on a holiday. He had seen her, heard
her talking Czech, and fallen in love with
her. He had introduced himself and followed
them like a shadow for two days; then they
had gone home. Soon afterwards he also
left; he took no further pleasure in his
surroundings. He had learned that the
gentleman was a manufacturer from one of

the larger towns in Bohemia, the girl was his daughter. After a little while he purposely visited their town and ventured to call on the family. He was received with civility—no more. The girl was a distinguished personality, but she was very cold. Her eyes had plainly shown him her astonishment when he presented himself : ' Does our accidental meeting in Dresden give you the right to follow me to the bosom of my family ? ' they seemed to say.

He went away, and a week later boldly asked for her hand. He wrote to her and to her father at the same time. The father's letter was very polite ; he evaded the disagreeable duty of a direct answer by the promise that his daughter herself should send the decision.

She had decided. Graciously but firmly she rejected his proposal.

' Well, that's finished,' Hron said to himself, ' now I must leave it alone. I suppose I am not important enough for her.'

But then the unexpected thing had happened : he saw from the newspapers six months later that her father's business had failed.

This news produced a strange sensation in Ivan Hron. He could have shouted for joy. How would his chances stand now ? He

returned to the town where they lived to
repeat his offer personally.

How embarrassed they had been when he
appeared ; almost as if they were ashamed of
themselves ! Hron told them as tactfully as
possible that his position would assure their
daughter a life free of cares, and all the
comforts she had been used to in her own
home.

The girl had seemed almost in despair.
This time her father spoke for her. He did
not refuse Hron's offer, but asked for a respite :
' Wait a month or two . . . or perhaps six
months ; have patience,' he said. ' You do
not know how much we all have suffered ;
everything is changed. And we have to see
to many things. I know you are a generous
man, you have proved it by returning now
that we are in trouble. It is not every man
who thinks as you do.'

Ivan Hron did wait for a whole six months ;
after that he wrote again, urgently, almost
imploringly. It was not the general manager
of an important banking combine who spoke
in these letters, but a young enthusiast. And
Magda became his own. Her father wrote
to him that she consented. Then Hron had
married her.

Later on he often thought of all this, and of the strange circumstances with which his suit and marriage had been attended. Had not fate in the first instance pointed out his way? Ought he not to have buried his hopes after that first refusal? Perhaps he would have found a girl equally beautiful, gentle and distinguished who would have made him wholly happy. . . .

He was always seized with a feeling of unspeakable sorrow when he arrived at this thought. Had Magda unconsciously had premonitions which had made her stand out against the marriage? Did she guess that she would never make her husband entirely happy? Was it a conviction that she would remain childless?

Then it would be she who was at fault!

Ivan Hron was almost maddened by his pondering and brooding at times. But tenderest compassion and deep pain filled his heart when, sometimes, late at night after having finished some important piece of work, he entered their bedroom on tiptoe. Before opening the door he would listen whether he could hear her sobbing. Then he would wait for hours until the spasm subsided, creep to his bed like a thief, relieved when he heard

her breathing quietly, and in the morning
when he waked her with a kiss, express in it
his whole love and tenderness. And when
his wife returned his embrace so warmly and
gratefully, she seemed to be asking his forgiveness. When he looked at her as she went
about her occupations and duties during the
day with care and thoughtfulness, he fell in
love with her afresh, and kissed her as on
that first day when he had taken her to their
new home. Therefore the constant recurrence
of the thought : ' How much happier we
might be if there were yet another being to
care for . . .' was all the more painful to him.

One beautiful afternoon in the summer Ivan
returned home earlier than usual from his
office. As he had his own latchkey he had no
need to ring the bell, and entered unobserved.
He put his hat and stick down in his study,
and went towards his wife's room. He did
not hear his own step on the thick carpet.
. . . Magda had not heard it either.

She hardly had time between the moment
of his opening the door and coming up to her,
to fold up a letter which she had been reading, and slip it into the envelope. She did
it quietly, and Hron did not notice that her

hands were trembling. When he was by her
side, she leant her left hand with the letter
in it on the table, and smoothed down something in her dress with the right hand, thus
keeping both her hands occupied. He could
not have failed to feel them trembling if he
had touched them.

'You've had a letter?' asked Ivan, pointing
to the envelope which peeped out from beneath
her fingers; he bent down to kiss her.

Every drop of blood ebbed from her face
when her lips met those of her husband; her
half-extinguished 'Yes' was lost in her kiss.

'From home?' he continued, looking at
the stamp, 'what news?'

Involuntarily he stretched out his hand for
the letter. At that moment Mrs Hron felt as
though she must run away or throw herself
out of the window, . . . but if she would
avoid a catastrophe she must do nothing to
rouse his suspicion. Her fingers painfully un-
clasped, but leant the more heavily on the table.

Hron took up the letter.

'That looks like a weekly review,' he said
good-humouredly, feeling it with his fingers,
'have you read it?' He half pulled the
letter from the envelope, and recognized his
mother-in-law's handwriting.

'Not quite,' answered the young woman. She tried to speak as audibly as she could, but her voice failed her, and her husband began to open the sheets which enclosed another sheet of paper.

'Well, the volumes you write to them are not much shorter,' he said kindly, and looked at her before he quite unfolded the letter.

She was standing upright, looking upon his hands with fear in her eyes, and was as white as chalk. Her fixed eyes did not take in her husband's astonishment.

Ivan Hron did not understand; but he thought he did. He suddenly remembered that she never touched his letters, however long they might have been lying on his writing-table: that she never even read a postcard addressed to him; she never showed the least curiosity about his correspondence. He had returned this reticence with regard to her letters. He never touched them without first asking: 'May I?' To-day he had failed to do this . . . she had not even finished reading the letter . . . he had broken the custom which had become a tacit understanding between them. That must be the cause of her astonishment and consternation. Therefore Ivan Hron folded the sheet up again, put it back into the envelope which he laid down on the table, and said in a conciliatory tone : 'Forgive me, Magda, that was not right.'

His wife forced herself to a gentle smile to conceal her terror, and it was a little while before she was able to say : ' You know it is from our people, nothing of importance, nothing new.'

She at once turned the conversation : ' You are early to-day ; has anything happened ? '

' What should have happened ? ' said her husband, ' I hurried home because I hoped we might get a walk. It is such lovely weather. If you feel inclined, we might go to the Sophia Island. Will you get ready ? '

Whistling softly to himself, he went to his room to wash his hands and put on fresh cuffs.

When he had gone, his wife opened a drawer of her bureau which contained her most precious and valuable possessions, took out a small box of cedarwood, locked the letter up in it, put the key in her pocket, and went out to dress.

They went down the staircase together and out into the street, where Hron offered his arm to his wife. He was delighted to feel how firmly she put her hand on his arm and pressed close to him. Yes, this arm was her hold and firm protection in this world !

Ivan Hron had no idea of what was passing in her mind.

A few days after this incident, which had passed entirely from Hron's memory, he was left alone in the house. He was planning his annual holiday outside Bohemia with his wife, and according to their custom Magda always went home to her parents for a few days first. They were now old, and she wished to see them and have the satisfaction of having been with them once more.

In her absence Ivan made preparations for their departure. His leave had begun already, and he spent his days at home. He locked up things that were to be left behind, and put everything in order. The next day Mrs Hron was to return from her native town.

Ivan Hron came home from his dinner at a restaurant, and began to pack his handbag. Then he went through all the rooms to see whether he had forgotten anything. He went into his wife's room, and smiled, noticing the order and neatness of everything.

Suddenly his eye was caught by her walnut bureau. All the drawers were locked except

the top one which had been pushed back
hastily.

'Just fancy, all her treasures unlocked,' he
thought: 'the room is not locked either; the
servant might have put her nose into everything.'

Involuntarily and without a set purpose,
he took hold of the two ornamental bronze
rings and pulled out the drawer.

In it were books, jewelry, embroideries,
photographs, and keepsakes. A box of cedarwood was in the right-hand corner. He knew
it; he himself had given it her as a Christmas
or New Year's present, when she had expressed
a wish for a box in which to keep various
trifles.

Hron touched the little box, and noticed
that the key of wrought iron was in it.

'Careless little woman! The drawer open
and the key in her box! And what about all
those sacred secrets, those valueless, and yet
so carefully guarded mysteries?'

It suddenly struck him, although he did
not feel the ordinary human curiosity: 'I
wonder what they are, these things that my
dear Magda has collected in this box?'

He almost smiled at the thought that
perhaps his first letter was among them, the

one which she had answered with a refusal?
As though this thought had with lightning-
speed been transferred to his hand, he touched
the key, turned it and opened the lid. The
remembrance of the letter, the answer to which
had poisoned six months of his life, was now
really exciting his curiosity. Had Magda
kept it? He himself was keeping her answer
in a drawer of his writing-table. Tactless or
not . . . he wanted to know! The little
box was filled with receipts and papers of
various kinds; on the top was the letter which
he had recently held in his hand and returned
to his wife. He recognized it by the handwriting and the date on the postmark. But
the letter had not been entirely slipped into
the envelope, a corner of it was peeping out;
Magda had probably read it several times,
and put it back loosely. Another letter was
folded into the large sheets which were covered
with his mother-in-law's handwriting, well
known to him. Hron could only see the
endings of words which were written in an
unknown, undeveloped hand.

He did not know why he did it, as he was
in fact looking for something else, but he
pulled out the sheet which was covered on
all its four pages with sprawling, large letters.

It was the attempt of a hand still awkward, and not much used to writing fluently. Irregular letters . . . the difference of thickness in the up- and down-strokes carefully observed . . . only children write like that. Which of the relatives . . . ?

He opened the sheet and read :

'MY BELOVED MUMMY,—How good of you to let me write to you again. I would like to write to you every day to tell you that I think of you and pray for you, because the clergyman tells us at school that we must pray for our parents. But as I cannot pray for Papa who is dead, I pray for my dear Mama whom I love so much, and I wish she were with me, because I cannot be with her. I do not know why I cannot be with her, when every daughter is with her mother. I know I cannot be with my Papa when he is dead, but why not with my Mama ? And when you say you love me, why do you not take me with you ? When I ask the lady, she tells me that the gentleman would not like it. What gentleman would not like it ? I think you must be in service like other mothers, and so you cannot have me with you, and I am so sorry I do not know where you are either.   My beloved Mummy, I would hide in a corner and keep quite quiet, so as not to worry the gentleman, and all day long I would not come out of my corner and the gentleman need not see me, and would not scold you, because he would not know I was there.   But at night, when you go to your little room I would kiss you, and sleep in your bed, and pray for you and your gentleman as I do now.   I could go to school, the same as I do here, and you should be pleased with me, for I like my lessons, and I am going to be moved to a higher standard again.   Oh my beloved mother, I should so like to have a photo of you ; the lady has photos of her sisters and aunts and other relations.   When the other lady came, who is my grandmother, I asked her for one, but she said I could not have it, because you had not got one.   And she told me I must be good, or else I must never write to you or see you again.   I cried very much, because I only see you once a year, and then I would never see you at all. My grandmother too cried, and said I might write to you again, that you had allowed it, and grandmother will come for this letter and send it to you, for little girls cannot send letters off by themselves, grandmother says.

'Dearest Mummy, come again, and come and see me on my birthday, which is on the feast of St. Peter and St. Paul ; I shall be eleven. I kiss your hand and am your obedient daughter,   MAGDA.

'*June 15th.*'

Ivan Hron had read the letter thinking that it must have got by mistake into the envelope which bore his wife's address. But when he arrived at the signature ' Magda,' he started. His heart beat with the sudden shock. He felt an unusual wave of heat mount to his head and flood his cheeks. A thought struck him which was so strange that he was startled afresh, and tried not to finish it. He quickly took up the second letter in his mother-in-law's handwriting. He devoured its contents, and large drops of perspiration were standing on his forehead, as though he were running a race. He felt his feet giving way beneath him, and sat down to finish the letter. There was nothing suspicious in it, the usual home news, good advice, inquiries, remembrances to her husband and thanks for his last contribution to the household expenses. Only quite at the end : ' I am sending you this letter which

you will like to see, and am your loving
mother. . . .' `

There it was ! That was the reference to
the letter !

Ivan Hron wiped his forehead and read his
mother-in-law's letter again, and then that
of little eleven-years-old Magda. His wife's
name !

He re-read it with the utmost attention.

Now, alas ! he understood ; but he also
felt as though his head would burst. His
Magda, his wife is little Magda's . . . impossible !

He sprang to his feet, caught up the little
box, and went to his room with it. He locked
the door, so as not to be disturbed, and hastily
turned out the contents : letters, photographs,
empty envelopes. But in spite of his eager-
ness he was careful to put them down in their
proper order, so that nothing should betray
afterwards that he had read anything. He
felt like a criminal while he was following up
Magda's secret. But even if it should be a
crime, he was going to commit it !

His hands were trembling feverishly, as he
went through the papers ; he took all his
father- and mother-in-law's letters out of
their envelopes, read them at a glance . . .

288 E³

nothing, nothing! Suddenly he came upon another letter written in the sprawling hand . . . a second . . . a third.

There were no more. The one which he had read first was the longest. The others were the more unlettered the older their date. Hron understood; as she made greater progress at school she was the more able to express her thoughts; her letters became longer, more legible, more appealing. From each of the four letters spoke the longing of this unknown child to see her mother, to be with her always. This incoherent babbling, these laboured sentences were the expression of a homesick child, praying for the fulfilment of its dearest wish.

Hron sat quite still and reflected painfully; his thoughts were like red-hot wires that penetrated his brain. 'My Magda . . . my Magda!' recurred over and over in his reflections, 'and then this child, this second Magda. . . .'

He recalled the moment when he had seen Magda for the first time, remembered how he had wooed her and been refused, and finally accepted. What had happened between the moment when he had first met her and the day when he had at last taken her to his home?

And suddenly Hron turned to his wife's little box again. Did it contain nothing else? Would he find the explanation of this terrible calamity? He remembered that the salesman had drawn his attention to the double bottom when he had bought the box; he had forgotten the contrivance, but now he tried hastily to discover the little hiding-place. He removed the sides, pulled out two ornamental rosettes and . . . there was the bottom. In it were some faded papers, covered with writing . . . in Magda's hand. They looked like the beginnings of letters, or notes from a diary; loose leaves, torn out of a book.

Hron began to read these sheets; the handwriting varied considerably, they had evidently been written at odd moments on various occasions. He read, and almost forgot to breathe. These leaves were the outpourings and anguished cries of a woman's soul in despair. If he had had any doubt as to the relationship of the two Magdas, these lines removed them. He saw the whole situation clearly. . . . What a fearful discovery! His own, his adored Magda!

Some of the sheets were quite fragmentary:
' There are worse things than death,' began

one, ' and I am on the rack. Everything
that I possessed in life has been destroyed
. . . our good name, my father's position
after a life of hard work . . . all in one blow.
The fruits of his labour are lost. But, terrible
as these losses are—all the more because of
their suddenness—they do not shatter me.
I wish they did !

' But my fate is more terrible than this ;
that of my parents is its crowning disaster.
The shame, oh the shame ! Never-ending
shame clings to my wasted life !

' It was all like a horrible, fantastic dream :
but the crying of the little creature whom
they have separated from me, the crying that
I heard for a moment only, which was lost
in the distance when they carried the little
girl away, this crying was the proof of a dreadful reality.

' And Robert does not return ! He has
disappeared, and gives no sign of whether he
is alive or dead. Alas ! my fall should have
helped him to rise, but then came my father's
failure . . . and what can be my value now ?
Did ever two more terrible misfortunes meet ? '

Another sheet began :

' He does not return. Perhaps he is seeking
death, perhaps he may have found it. The

misery of it ! He is a coward ; it would have needed energy on his part to begin life afresh, and his life would have given me back my life also. What a fate, to have been betrayed by a mountebank ! But the most terrible thing about it is that that other man who came into my life, is again offering me his hand and asking for mine. I am in despair. I resist all I can, but there is my father, who is looking so ill ; he does not say anything, but his dear old eyes make such an eloquent appeal . . . my mother was on her knees before me, wringing her hands and entreating me : Don't refuse him . . . consent !

'This other, good, honest man is to be deceived. My parents entreat me that it should be so. Shall I give in to their appeal ? Shall I make up my mind to hide from him what sort of a wife he wishes to marry ?

'And to be separated for ever from that innocent creature . . . disavow her for ever ! For she will not die. I am sure my parents are praying that she might be taken, but my prayers are stronger, and she will live ! I keep on praying that she will live. . . .'

Again on another sheet :

'The decision has been made ; my conscience has tormented me from the moment when my

father said " Yes " for me. Do I care for
him ? Have I a right to say I love the man
whom I approach with a lie ? How can I
bear his eyes, how shall I breathe in his
embraces ?

' They have tormented me, forced my
hands ! They took away my child, I do not
know where she is. I want to see her . . . I
am dying with longing to kiss her, press her
to my heart . . . where is she ?

' They promised that I should see her if I
consented to marry him. My child, what a
price to pay for your kisses ! Unfortunate
Ivan ! What a price for you to pay for me
. . . how you are being deceived. . . .'

On the last sheet, on which the first lines
had been crossed out, he read :

' To-morrow is my wedding day . . . I feel
as though it were my funeral. Alas ! I feel
something is being carried to its grave. . . .
I myself am burying it. I am murdering my
peace of mind . . . perhaps I am also
murdering Ivan's happiness.

' And my father and mother kiss me and
embrace me. Neither of them says a word
about it, but their eyes are saying a great
deal. They are grateful to me that I have
yielded, that I have consented to . . . sell

myself. I cannot express what I feel when I see Ivan, full of love, beaming with happiness because I am to be his. . . .

‘ There is one thought of comfort in these bitter, desperate hours for which I am thanking heaven : Robert is dead. He has gone out of my life ; his shadow will never fall between Ivan and me, he will never come back.

‘ I do not know if the moment will ever come when I shall dare to say that I love Ivan. I tremble when I think of his asking me whether I love him. And perhaps he will ask me to-morrow . . . to-morrow ! But the thought that that coward is dead is balm to my soul.’

Ivan Hron had finished the perusal of the papers ; he breathed a sigh of relief. After what he had read, this fact that the unknown father of little Magda was no longer alive, was a load off his mind. He was breathing audibly, like a man waking up out of a heavy sleep.

‘ Whoever he was, he is dead now. . . .’

Ivan Hron stared at the sheets and fragmentary notes in front of him with burning eyes ; then he slowly put his elbows on to the table and buried his head in his hands ; his soul had been profoundly stirred, and a painful sob broke from his compressed throat. A moment later his whole body, his shoulders and hands and head began to tremble, and large tears fell upon the faded, traitorous leaves.

It did not occur to him to think of how long it was since he had cried, nor that he was a strong man with experience of life, and that he ought not to give way ; he only felt a fearful scorching pain, such as he had felt once before in his life at the time when he had been banished from his home on account of his ill-considered youthful exploit. But at that time he had been young, and the whole world lay open before him. He had then sustained an irreparable loss, but from the depth of his despair he looked for the dawn of a future. What was left to him now ? He was now living that future to which he had been looking forward then ; he had climbed to the summit of his life, there was no going higher or further. His daily life was circumscribed, there would be no great changes either in his career or in his home ; he had come to the limits of both. He was at the head of his office and he was married ; this was the last stage of his life, and though it might go on for another ten or

twenty years, it would always be the same.
He would get older, one day he would retire;
there were no other prospects. He well knew
the limits within which he was living, and
now, just as he was approaching their border,
this thing happened, to poison both the past
and the future for him !

Ivan Hron wept for a long time, until his
tears naturally ceased to flow. Only now and
then convulsive spasms betrayed his inward
crying. But even the spasms became less
frequent; there was a sob from time to time,
and at last a silence.

He sat for a while, supporting his head in
his hand. He did not realize how great the
relief had been which his tears had given him.
When he raised his head, his tears had ceased
to flow, only his eyes were a little swollen and
inflamed. The expression of his face was
calm; the storm had passed. He looked as
though he had resigned himself to an irreparable, unalterable fate.

He took his pocket-handkerchief and wiped
his eyes; then he quietly replaced the sheets
of papers, letters, photographs and trifles in
the box in their proper order. Nothing should
betray their having been touched by an
unauthorized hand. When he took up little

Magda's fateful letter, which had so recently
caused him the bitterest moment of his life,
he glanced once more at the lines written by
this unknown, pining little creature. Now he
could enter into it much more. Alas ! How
much bitterness this little heart had already
had to taste ! But how great must have been
the pain that his wife had suffered all the time
since she had been tied to him and separated
from her child . . . day by day, whole
months, years . . . ten long years. What
fortitude this delicate woman had shown in
mastering herself and enduring the separation
. . . or was she upheld by some hope ? What
was this hope ?

Hron stopped short at the words : ' Dearest
Mummy, come again, come on my birthday,
on the day of St. Peter and St. Paul. . . .'

Yes, Magda had complied with her wish.
It was a week since she went away, and to-day
was St. Peter and St. Paul. At the moment
when her fateful secret had revealed itself to
him accidentally, a little creature in some
distant place was laughing with joy at her
mother's embrace, and his wife was happy
in the presence of her growing daughter,
answering her thousand questions, asking a
thousand herself, kissing her, kissing her for a

whole year. But in the midst of all this love
and tenderness the clock would strike merci-
lessly, the day would wane, and Magda press
her child closer and yet closer . . . her child,
from whom she must tear herself after a few
hours, to be separated again for a whole year.
And even if she should think of him, her
husband, how bitter must that thought be to
her! She would have to return to him without betraying by a single word what she had
gone through. Her heart would break with
the pain of another separation, yet she might
not complain; she must master herself with
all her strength, so as not to arouse his suspicion. Where would her thoughts be before
she returned to him, when he would press her
to his heart and kiss her? Every caress
which he had taken to himself had really been
meant for her little daughter. When she
passed her hand over his head she probably
thought of her. And perhaps she hoped to
win his forgiveness at the moment when he
might discover her secret, with the care,
tenderness and attention which she had given
him. Did she dread that moment? Surely,
it must haunt her!

Ivan's heart was caught up in a feeling of
unbounded pity. The feeling which was

uppermost in his mind was not that he had
been deceived, but that he had been excluded
from a triple alliance.

Slowly he folded up the letter and put it,
and what was left of other things, back into
their place, and carried the box to Magda's
room. He carefully replaced it in the drawer,
which he locked, so that Magda should have no
idea that her carelessness had induced any one
to open it.

As he left the room, he happened to look
into a glass, and noticed his inflamed, swollen
eyes. He hurried into his room, poured water
into his basin, adding a little lavender water,
and sponged and dried his face. When he
had done this and brushed his dishevelled hair,
Hron slowly changed his clothes. The large,
empty rooms seemed lonely, and he felt that
he must get away from them into the fresh
air, to some place where he would not be
likely to meet many people. He could not
bear the idea of seeing any one he knew; he
wanted to be alone, to reflect, to work out
this problem and come to a resolution. He
locked his wife's room and put the key in his
pocket, in case the servant should spy upon
her secret in his absence. How glad he was
that that moment had found him alone; he

had allowed the girl to go to a procession. No one had surprised him, no one knew that anything had happened.

He slowly went down the stairs. His thoughts were moving round and round in a strange circle.   A picture of Doré's from the *édition de luxe* of his Bible occurred to him ; it represented the expulsion from paradise.   As he left his house he felt as though he too were being driven from his paradise.   Day by day he had hastened hither to meet his beloved Magda.   He thought of her return the next day and shivered.   How would he feel at meeting her ?   Would he be able to master his features sufficiently for her not to see that he now knew what she had kept a secret for so long, what perhaps she had meant to keep a secret for ever ?   What kind of a life between them would it be if Magda discovered *his* secret ?

If only he could escape meeting friends to-day !   He wished he were a stranger to all the world.

He went to a part of Prague where he had hardly ever been before, across the ' little bridge ' and through the passages of the crooked old town on the banks of the Moldavia. It was a fine day ; all those who could walk had left the streets behind; Hron met only a few strangers. The place seemed almost deserted. He crossed the river by the stone bridge and turned through a side-street towards the Bruska. But that was full of people, so he went through the archway and out into the fields.

He breathed a sigh of relief when he was there, but the consciousness of his sorrow did not leave him. He thought of his wedding-day and his married life. His thoughts came and went incoherently; he thought of the time before his marriage. Who was this man who had been the first to win Magda's heart, her whole heart, even herself? Who was he, the father of Magda, who was dead? When had all that happened? And again he felt the tears rising in his throat, and an immeasurable pain, as though he had lost what he treasured most. But at that time . . . Magda had not been his! He also thought of the moments when their child-lessness had been most bitter to him; when he had looked enviously at his friends' families and their happiness, when he had romped with their children. Now he understood Magda's mute, eloquent looks on those occasions, which had haunted him. ' If that were my

child ! ' she must have thought. Yes : she
was thinking of her own child who was
living hidden, a stranger among strangers,
uncaressed, without a father, and deprived of
her mother too during all the years when she
most needed her. That was what her looks
meant . . . it was that . . . that ! At
moments when Hron had caressed other
children her thoughts, with all the suppressed,
secret mother-instinct fled to her own lonely
little daughter whom she dared not acknowledge, of whom she might not be proud, whom
she might not kiss before all the world, nor
dress her, nor take her to school, whom she
could not tuck up at night, nor prepare Santa
Claus surprises for her, and taste that sweetest
of all joys, that of seeing a little face beam
with delight. The child had been robbed of
everything, and so had she. What an un-
ending atonement ! She had a child which
she could not take into her own home. He
felt that it was only now that he knew her
really, and in spite of all the bitterness which
filled his heart he sighed : ' Poor Magda ! '
Magda had a child ! Hron suddenly stopped
dead ; his thoughts glanced off in another
direction. She *had* a child !

Ivan Hron took off his hat, wiped his

forehead and looked straight in front of him at the green field. But he did not know what he was looking at, he was looking inwards. All the morbid moments of his brooding on the problem of their childlessness passed before his soul. He remembered how he had tormented himself to find the cause of it. And his wife had had . . . she had a child !

He stood, drawing deep breaths.

What was passing in Madga's mind, if she saw through him ? Did she guess that he suspected the fault to be hers ? And she had to bear the blame in silence.

He was overcome by remorse. He now realized fully how difficult the moment of their meeting would be.

Ivan Hron started off again along the edge of the field ; he did not care whither he was going, he only sought for an escape from the labyrinth of his thoughts. He counted neither moments nor hours, he did not know how long he had been wandering about, when the setting sun reminded him that night was approaching.

He turned back towards Prague hurriedly, without minding by which road he went, noticing nothing by the way. From the

Belvedere he turned to cross the Francis-Joseph bridge.

Not till he had reached the narrow Elisabeth Street did he become conscious of ordinary daily life again. He glanced at the two rows of high houses with their countless windows, and the thought struck him :

' Now, this is only a small fraction of a big town, yet what a multitude of little unimportant human beings, what life-stories, problems, emotions and struggles lie hidden behind all those windows, in all the rooms inhabited by people ; under the roofs of the splendid mansions with balconies as well as under those of back-alleys. And when these struggling souls come out into the streets, they hide what is passing in them.'

He was suddenly seized by a fear that some one might guess from his looks how miserable, humbled and desperate he felt. No ! Only he himself should know what had happened to him ; no one should stand still and look after him, pitying him and thinking : ' Poor Hron, whatever is the matter with him ? ' As though he had not a trouble in the world, Hron pulled down his waistcoat, looked at his watch, felt whether he had a cigar with him, lit it deliberately, and walked towards Joseph's Square.

Along the narrow Elisabeth Street human life had flowed like a stream, but in Joseph Square it expanded in broad billows like a sea. All the excursionists converged hither to be scattered in all directions. The trams were rattling past, making the flag-stones tremble. Almost forgetting his troubles, he looked at the crowds which were storming the cars. These people, battling for room to sit or stand in them, seemed to him like lunatics. They fought their way with their elbows, pushed others off the steps to mount in their place; some positively butted into a medley of bodies and limbs, and others who had already boarded a car, were suddenly seized with fear and tried to alight again. Hats fell from their heads; some caught their dresses, and the seams of their garments were strained to the utmost, or gave way.

'What do they mean by it?' thought Hron, 'why this wild struggle?'

The gas-lamps were beginning to sparkle . . . one . . . another . . . a third. Ivan Hron watched the lamplighter with his pole who went regularly from post to post with his head bent, and without minding the wild tumult. A yellow mail-cart rattled past ; the full letter boxes of the whole town would now yield their contents. Bourgeois with their wives returned from their walks ; the women led the bigger children by the hand, the men carried the little ones. A detachment of firemen were crossing the street. The police were changing patrols.

Ivan felt that there was something restful to his mind in all this noise and movement, rattling and crowding. By degrees he became calmer. His senses, strained to breaking point by the great shock, relaxed and were able to take in other impressions. He put his hat, which had slipped back, straight, and walked more firmly.

' Forget it all . . . at least for a while, for to-night ! '

He made up his mind to join a party of his friends at a restaurant, so as to change his thoughts. He absolutely must think of something else, he had brooded enough. He meant to drink a good deal. Many people cure their troubles with wine ; he too would try this remedy. He must avoid being alone in the empty house ; he must take home an atmosphere of conviviality, else he would feel suffocated. And Hron went into a restaurant where he would be sure to meet friends.

But Ivan was one of those men who did not easily get drunk; his strong head could always master the effect of the wine, and he did not care to drink far beyond his measure. Yet the wine cheered him; he listened to the talk and gossip, and forced himself to join in it. He spent several hours in this noisy company, and received his friends' respectful remembrances to his wife almost cheerfully. It was past midnight when he returned home. The servant was snoring in her bedroom next the kitchen. Ivan gently locked the door and went through the hall on tiptoe. He found a letter from his wife on the table; she let him know by which train she intended to arrive. He lit the candles in his bedroom and went to bed with a book. But he had not been reading many lines when his hands with the book slowly dropped on the coverlet, and he looked across at the portrait of his wife over the chesterfield. For nearly an hour he lay quite still, looking fixedly at the lovely face which was so dear to him. He was painfully winning through to a resolution. Presently his lips moved without a sound, framing the words : ' It shall be so.'

Perhaps he hardly heard them himself; he
had instinctively given form to the last link
in the chain of his thoughts, which might
prove a solution of the problem.

Then he sat up in bed and put out both
candles in the branch-candlestick. When he
lay back in his pillows he whispered reproach-
fully : ' Magda, Magda ! '

Magda Hron had told her husband that she
would arrive on the last day of June by the
afternoon train. Ivan was thankful that it
would be in the later part of the day, almost
in the evening ; he would have the whole day
to set his mind in order, as he said to himself.

He had hoped for this when he had returned
from the restaurant the night before. But
apparently the setting in order took him a
shorter time than he had anticipated. Although
he had been out unusually late the night
before and had not gone to sleep for a good
while, he awoke at an early hour and got up
at once. He looked thoughtful but calm, his
face betrayed no trace of yesterday's struggle.
The storm had passed, his resolution held firm.

What was his resolution ? Was he going
to put his wife away ? Or induce her to
consent to a separation with maintenance for

her and her daughter ? This thought had
occurred to him, but had been rejected at
once. He realized that he could not hope to
redeem his over-insistence in the past, nor
ought to punish his wife by bringing an action.
He was a prominent man, and his position
would not stand a scandal ; but apart from
that, what would he gain by violent measures ?
Would he be the happier for them ? Would
they not utterly destroy his future life ? Was
it likely that Magda would be happy, if the
moment which restored her to her daughter
were to rob her of her husband and home ?
And even if she should bear this fate without
murmuring, could he live without her after the
ten years of purest harmony between them, and
when he loved her as much now as when he
took her to his house for the first time ? Nay
. . . since yesterday he loved her with a
passion which was mingled with pain ; when
he had learnt that he had a rival in the child,
he had begun to tremble for his place in her
heart.

Hron's struggle was over, he looked composed. He dressed quickly, breakfasted, and
told the servant at what time her mistress
would return, and what she was to prepare,

lit his cigar and left the house. It was too early to go to his office, so he decided to go for a walk. A stroll without a set purpose on this warm, sunny morning of the departing June would strengthen yesterday's resolution; he would breathe the fresh air, look at happy faces of people who went in all directions about their daily duties, taking them up at the point where they had left them yesterday, and trying not to show traces of intervening struggles.

He passed the Girls' High School. It was nearly eight o'clock, the children were hurrying to school. Many of them were accompanied by servants, elder sisters, or mothers. Hron stood still and from a distance watched the mothers taking leave of their darlings. They bent over them, gave them last instructions, then they kissed them lovingly and looked after them till they had disappeared in the school-entrance and winding corridors. His Magda would do the same; he knew she would not leave the child until she was quite sure she was safe. There was a faint smile on Hron's face when this thought crossed his mind like a flash. The stream of children was ebbing away: now it had been absorbed by the school-house. Only a few late-comers ran in quickly, afraid of missing the beginning of the lesson ; at last the place was completely deserted. Hron walked on towards his office.

The hours were all too slow for him that day. He could hardly wait for his wife's return. He went to the Sophia Island, to dine in company with a few friends whose families were already in the country.

' Still a grass-widower ? ' some of them asked him.

' Only till to-night,' he answered with a smile, ' my wife will return this afternoon from her visit to her parents ; then it will be only a few days before we are off on our holiday somewhere. Our boxes are ready to be packed.'

' Where are you going, Direktor ? '

' Perhaps to Berlin and Hamburg on the way to Heligoland, or a quiet seaside place like Travemünde, perhaps in the other direction, to Munich, Salzburg and the Alpine Lakes. I don't know yet, I shall see what my wife proposes.'

Hron was absent-minded at dinner and hurried away soon after, as though he were afraid to miss the train. He gulped down his cup of black coffee and went home. He

opened the windows in his wife's room and in
the dining-room, so that she should not find
them stuffy on her return.   He put a bunch
of fresh flowers into the bedroom, carnations
and roses, which he had bought on his way
home.   He locked her room, told the servant
to have dinner ready at seven o'clock, and
loitered   towards   his   office,   although   the
official hour had not yet struck, as though he
could hurry on the clock.   He could hardly
contain himself.

But the nearer six o'clock and with it her
arrival approached, the more uneasy he became, as if after all he dreaded their meeting.
He was grateful to the chief cashier for joining
him as far as the station when he left the
Bank ; he did not wish to be alone.   And
when the cashier had left him, he was drawn
into a vortex of departing and arriving people ;
he felt dazed with the perpetual ringing of
bells, shouting of the staff, thundering of
trains which arrived from both directions.
Yet he welcomed the infernal noise ; it
would sufficiently absorb Magda's senses not
to make her look too closely at his features,
and discover the emotion which had flushed
his cheeks.

Then her train was signalled, and rolled

into the station a few minutes later. He at
once saw her, as she was alighting. A slight
trembling seized him, a few steps brought
him near to her. The blood mounted to her
face. He was relieved that he had to turn
and speak to a porter before addressing
her. Magda took his arm and walked on
quickly, almost drawing him forward; she
was looking straight ahead. Her cheeks were
almost on fire. Hron did not guess or understand that she too always suffered from great
nervousness when she met him again for the
first time. She was almost dying with fear
that she might betray in some way whence she
came and of what nature her visit had been.
All her attention was fixed on guarding her
secret, lest her husband should suspect her.
But he had pressed her hand and drawn it
closer . . . no, he suspected nothing! She
was breathing more freely while he was helping
her to get into the carriage, and while the
wheels were rattling over the cobblestones.
Saved once more!

'Well, Magda,' said Hron, breaking the
silence which had reigned between them since
they had got into the carriage, and was
beginning to frighten him, 'have you had a
good time? No disappointments?'

' Excellent, Ivan, everything went right,' answered his wife.

' You found them all well ? '

' Yes, quite. Father had not been well about a month ago. They did not tell me, because they did not want me to be anxious. But he is better, he is really quite well again.'

' You found it hard to part with them, didn't you, Magda ? ' said Hron.

The blood again mounted to Magda's cheek. Her eyes became fixed, and did not meet his. Oh, how hard it had been to part with that little creature ! But she was obliged to give an answer.

' You know I am fond of my parents, and they are getting old ; every year is like a gift. And yet every year I leave them with the hope of seeing them the next.'

' And they have not yet made up their minds to come and live in Prague ? ' he asked. ' We would find a charming, cosy little nest for them and make them very comfortable. Haven't you tried to persuade them ? '

Hron made this proposal every year on Magda's return from her old home, but she shrank from it. She would indeed have liked to have her parents near her, but if they came to Prague, how could she see little Magda ? What pretext could she find ? Two kinds of love were ever struggling within her, but the stronger, the mother-love always won the day.

' You are so kind, Ivan,' she answered, ' but I don't think we shall persuade them. They are too old ; they had better stay in the surroundings in which they have lived all their lives ; they would hardly get used to the life in Prague. If anything happened to them they would be sure to think it was because they had left their old home. Besides, it would mean greater expense for you; as it is you are showing them so much kindness that I don't know how I can ever be grateful enough to you.'

She warmly pressed his hand.

Ivan Hron was unspeakably happy. He kept her hand in his and said gently : ' Be fond of me always, Magda. It is the sweetest gratitude you can give me.'

They were both silent after that for the few minutes which it took to reach their home.

Two days later the couple left Prague. Ivan was restless, but not because he wanted a change of scene. He was almost unwilling

to travel this year, indeed, quite unwilling.
He would have liked to have carried out his
plan at once, but he could not think of a
cogent reason to give to his wife for not going
for their usual trip. It was too late to pretend
that he could not get leave; everything had
been settled and prepared before Magda
started to go to her parents. And Magda
knew how he loved to travel. So they
started, and went as far as Munich.

Hron was hoping that in strange surroundings, away from the daily round, and among
strangers, he might more easily find an
opportunity of saying what he wanted to
say. On their travels, when they were closer
companions than usual, they were always
more tender, more intimate than at home.
Hron always felt as though they were lovers.

The opportunity for which he was longing
presented itself earlier than he thought. They
stayed in Munich for a week, and went for a
trip on the Stahrenberg Lake on their last
day. It was a lovely, sunny morning. A
light breeze was rippling the surface of the
lake, when they left the train at Stahrenberg,
to board the comfortable steamer 'Wittels-
bach.' Their first objective was charming
Leoni, where they ascended to the Rottmann's

Height, and enjoyed the lovely view over the distant Alps. After an hour and a half they returned to the landing-stage, to go further up the lake by another steamer. A small family, perhaps belonging to the villa-colony of Leoni, boarded the steamer 'Bavaria' at the same time; they were a young couple with two children, a boy of about three, a curly, sunburnt, restless little rogue, who ran about the deck like quicksilver, and a pale, almost transparent-looking girl of five, who was very much muffled up. It was easy to guess that this child with waxen cheeks had been racked by a severe illness quite recently, in fact, it had apparently not yet quite relaxed its hold upon the victim. The boy was looked after by a handsome, careful young girl, but the mother herself was nursing her little daughter, happy at being able to take her out on the lake again for the first time. She hardly took her eyes off the precious convalescent, at whose bed, no doubt, she had watched for whole nights with bitter tears and fervent prayers.

With her tired, hollow eyes the little girl was looking at the lake, beneath the opalescent surface of which slumbered the green depth. They were fixed on one spot, as though she were expecting to see mermaids rising from the water; she knew them well, her mother had often told her the story. Now and then the child coughed, and then the young mother would cover her throat more closely with the silk handkerchief, or wrap the small, pointed elbows round with a cloak. And a kiss would accompany each of these movements.

Ivan Hron was watching his wife . . . her eyes had been resting for a long time on the little girl, and returned to her over and over again. Ivan read what was passing in her mind : ' She is thinking of her little one.'

The lovely morning, the fresh strong air, the view of the distant Alps had attuned his soul to tenderness; he was more receptive, more sensitive than usual. He guessed his wife's thoughts : yes, she is thinking of her child. Her little Magda too might be taken with a severe illness, might be racked by fever. In her delirium she would call for her mother. Yet not her soft hand but a stranger's would minister to her; her mother dare not come. Perhaps in her last battle with death her dim eyes would be half opened to seek those she had loved above all things, her hands would be stretched out to embrace the head whose first and last thought was for her child . . .

in vain, in vain! And her last dying groan
would be wrung from her by the pain that
her little heart could not break at her mother's
breast.

Ivan Hron's eyes grew dim at this thought,
and as though their thoughts had met, he
heard a deep sigh which rose from his wife's
bosom.

He took her hand. 'You are looking at that
poor child, Magda, you are sorry for her . . .'

His wife did not answer; her eyes looked
into vacancy, her eyelids trembled.

'Yet how happy this child is, all the same,'
Ivan continued almost in a whisper. 'She is
carefully nursed, her mother watches her like
a guardian angel.'

Two large tears ran down Magdalena's
cheeks; she had not the courage to look at
her husband.

'Listen, Magda,' said Ivan, taking her hand,
'it has long been my intention to tell you
something; there are so many orphans who
do not belong to a soul in this world, who are
in want of what they most need, and do not
know what it means to be really loved and
cared for. And as we ourselves have not
been so fortunate as to have a family of our
own, and we have no children to consider,

could we not adopt one of those lonely children who have no home ? And it would be more lively for us, Magda. . . .'

Magda did not answer ; but the heaving of her breast showed the deep emotion in her soul, and what a storm of thoughts and conflicts her husband's words had roused.

' You do not answer, Magda, you do not agree ? You do not care about it ? '

' Do as you wish.' Her words were almost inaudible.

' Ah, I knew you would not thwart me, Magda,' said Ivan gently. ' And if you should be thinking about your people, believe me, in case I should die unexpectedly no one will be curtailed by this increase in our family. I have made provisions for everybody as well as you. Look,' he continued eagerly, ' some little boy who has neither father nor mother shall find them in us. Would you like me to look out for a curly little fellow like this one ? '

Magda's hand was trembling in his. ' As you like, Ivan ; yes, I agree.'

Ivan was silent, then he began again : ' Or would you rather have a little girl ? A little creature whose mind would begin to open out when she lived with us ; she would soon get used to us and would see her parents in us

. . . we could give her our names. You'd rather have a girl, wouldn't you, Magda? A girl is more domesticated; you could dress her, and make of her what you liked, give her mind its proper bent . . . yes, I think you would get more quickly used to a girl, wouldn't you?'

The young woman's eyes looked glassy, although the two tears on her cheeks had dried, But a fresh pain which would have no end was beginning to take possession of her soul. Her fixed eyes, unable to perceive anything in her immediate surroundings, looked into the far distance, and her heart went out in immeasurable sorrow, hunted to death. If ever she had dared to hope that the day might come when she could acknowledge little Magda, if ever a ray of hope had lighted up her soul . . . all that would be lost now. What she had felt for her own, what she would have done for her with her last breath, was now to be given to an unknown child. The place which she had dreamt of for the unfortunate little creature would never be taken by her. Oh, the pain of it! The awful punishment for a single moment of weakness, the endless atonement for the sin of another! Her Magda would now be really lost to her;

she would be for ever excluded from her rightful place.

The thought of humbling herself before her husband and revealing her secret, flashed through her mind. But she forced it away from her. Should she, at the moment when he was thinking of doing good and giving a home and parents to some unfortunate being, crush him with her dreadful disclosure ?

After a long pause, and without looking at him : ' Yes, do so,' she said in a whisper.

' You really mean it, and you don't even look at me ? ' said Hron as with a gentle reproach. ' I know it is hard to speak of these things, but I am afraid there is no prospect of a change. But all the same, if you do not like the idea. . . .'

When later on Magda remembered this moment, she was conscious of having fought a hard battle with herself for the second time in her life, just as hard as that after which she had consented to accept Ivan's hand. But she now had the strength to turn to him, and look at him with her brimming eyes, while her hand gently returned the pressure of his right hand. She said firmly : ' Not at all, I quite agree with you.'

The subject was not mentioned between

them again. The day was bright, and every-thing looked smiling, the rays of the July sun shone warm upon them, but they remained silent all day. The deep melancholy which had taken possession of her could not be banished from Magda's face. Hron at first tried to distract her, but ended by being lost in silent reflection too. For him also this afternoon's conversation had meant a hard struggle. He had prepared himself for many days, and every time he had meant to begin, the words had stuck in his throat. But in spite of his serious mood, he had a feeling of deep satisfac-tion, and if he had been a more introspective man, he would have said to himself that he was really immensely happy.

After this conversation with his wife, Ivan became restless. He shortened the remainder of their trip, hurried from place to place, and left unvisited some in which he had meant to make a stay. He often secretly watched Magda, and saw how she was suffering. She mastered herself with all her strength, tried to conquer the apprehension which Ivan's intention had roused in her, and even made attempts to appear gay. Perhaps she secretly clung to the hope that something would prevent the plan at the last moment. But

how could that be ? She could not tell. If
she were to change his mind in favour of her
daughter, she would have to speak. Could
that change possibly be in her child's and her
own favour ? Might she not be sent away with
her unfortunate child at once ? She could
do nothing. And Ivan, who read her thoughts,
became himself subject to depression. His
nature, more robust than hers, was not affected
as deeply as her sensitive soul, yet he became
more and more anxious to put an end to this
state of uncertainty. The solution of the
problem was in his hand, and he fervently
desired to solve it ; yet when he thought of
what it would mean, he trembled for Magda
and for himself.

In Salzburg rainy weather set in, which
gave him a pretext for returning to Prague
without delay. Magda did not seem to care
what they did ; nothing had appealed to her
on this journey, neither did she look forward
to going home. Dull indifference had now
taken possession of her. What did it matter
whether she were away or at home ? The
situation was desperate in any case. There
was no way out of the impasse. She strained
all her senses to get hold of an idea, but
none presented itself ; not a single flash

came to light up the heavy gloom of her horizon.

They were home again. Ivan Hron's leave had not yet expired. He went to his office to see whether there were news of any importance, but after he had settled that he need not resume his duties for another fortnight, he returned to his wife. On the next day he made preparations for another journey. 'I have to attend to some business in the country, Magda,' he said, 'I want to settle it while I am on leave. But I shall be back in a couple of days or so, and if you like we can then go for another trip. Perhaps a favourable wind may blow me in the direction of your home. I may see your parents; but I am not sure.'

When he took leave of her, with his bag in his hand, he remarked casually: 'Well, Magda, if I should find a little orphan by the wayside, you would not mind my bringing her along? It would be best to get one from the country; all her former ties, whatever they might be, would then be severed, and she would begin a new life in Prague. If you should not take to her, we will send her back.'

'Do as you think best,' said Magda with resignation. 'I am sure I shall approve of your choice; you are a man who can be trusted.'

' If I succeed, I will write and let you know,' said Hron, tenderly embracing his wife, and left the house.

Three days passed. Hron had not written. But on the morning of the fourth day she received a letter :

' DEAREST MAGDA,—I have found what I was looking for, a little girl without father and mother. She is not quite so small a child as you might fancy, but I hope you will take to her all the same. Meet us the day after to-morrow at the North Western Station at 1 p.m. Be sure to have dinner ready at once; we shall probably be hungry. Greatly looking forward to our meeting—Your

IVAN.'

Magda went towards the station to meet her husband, with a heavy heart. She walked up and down the platform, and her breath stopped when she heard the whistle of the approaching train. Immovable, as though she were rooted to the spot, the young woman stood, her eyes only were moving and wandered from one carriage to another, seeking the one from which her husband would alight with the child. But the passengers, each one looking for the friends or relatives who would meet them, passed her; one carriage after another discharged its occupants, and at last the train was empty; the doors stood out like wooden wings, the engine hissed feebly. Ivan was nowhere to be seen. He had not come.

Magda stood a little while longer, waiting to see if her husband would appear after all; at last she wondered whether she had made a mistake in the time. Having asked some questions from uncommunicative officials, which were not answered any too willingly, she returned home. The thought that something might have happened to her husband did not occur to her. She thought that she might not have read his note carefully enough, or that he had made a mistake in the time. Besides, she was too much engrossed in other things. Her thoughts were far away in a remote little village in the North-east of Bohemia with her Magda . . . her Magda who did not know that her place would now be taken by another child.

Magda had gone up the front door steps of her house and was pressing the electric bell.

How lonely the house had felt while Ivan had been away !

The door was opened at once, and . . . by Ivan himself. She was taken aback, almost startled, so that he had to draw her into the hall. He kissed her and said : ' You have had the trouble for nothing, Magda, forgive me. I altered my plans at the last moment, and we came by the main line. There was no time to let you know, so I was obliged to let you take a walk by yourself. But come in now, come and see. . . .'

' " We " came ! Then she is here ! '

Suddenly Magda's feet refused to move ; she tried in vain to follow her husband. He gently put his arm round her shoulders and led her, so that she was obliged to move forward. Half-leading, half-drawing her, he took her as far as the dining-room door which he opened. When he spoke encouragingly to her once more, there was a slight tremor in his voice. ' Come now, Magda,' he said, ' come and tell me if you are pleased with me.' He pushed her gently forward without releasing his hold upon her.

Magda looked into the room, where a shy little girl was sitting on the sofa. She looked startled, and perhaps a little frightened after

all the changes she had lived through during
the last two days. Her large brown eyes were
looking towards the door when she heard the
voice of the man whom she had only so lately
met for the first time. But when she saw
Magda appear on the threshold, she sprang
to her feet, her cheeks burned, and she cried :
' Mummy ! '

' Magda ! '

Magdalena's voice was choked, the last
syllable remained unspoken. The blood left
her face, her body was swaying. She clutched
the fingers of Ivan's right hand as though she
were drowning ; still she could not stand, and
sank down on her knees which had given way
beneath her.

' Magda,' cried Hron, trying to hold her up,
' pull yourself together, little mother.'

Magda resisted. Not standing . . . only
kneeling she could listen to the terrible things
which a deceived husband must now speak.

But his arms lifted her up completely, and
his right hand raised her head which had
dropped on to her chest.

' Magda,' he whispered, trembling all over,
' be brave, don't frighten our little daughter.'

He lifted her head almost by force, to look
into her eyes. But she had closed them ; a

deathly pallor had spread over her face, her teeth were chattering as in a fever. She could hardly utter the words : ' Who told you, Ivan, who told you ? '

' Nobody told me.' Hron passed his hand over her cold cheek. ' I want you to be perfectly happy, my dearest child. Now, please go and welcome the other Magda, else she will begin to cry. Come, little daughter, give your mother courage.'

The child hesitated for a moment, then she ran up to her mother, threw her arms round her body, and cried anxiously : ' Mummy, Mummy, what is the matter with you ? '

But Magda, before Ivan knew what she was doing, or could prevent it, had seized his right hand and pressed it to her lips. It was not till now that the truth flashed upon her. Ivan had brought this about, but not to accuse or punish her. Hot tears fell on his hands, and when at last he could take her head in both his hands to kiss her, her whole soul looked in gratitude out of her brimming eyes.

' Ivan . . . Ivan,' her lips trembled, ' do you think my whole life will be enough in return for what you are doing for this father- less child ? '

' What ? Fatherless ! ' Ivan cried gaily, so

as not to break down himself, ' she has had a
father for two whole days . . . he has been
found, he has come to claim her, here is
documentary evidence . . . look here.'

He put his hand in his breast pocket, drew
forth a document and waved it over her
head: 'While I was about it I have brought
Magda's christening certificate as well, so
now we can enter her at the High School
after the holidays. But enough of all this.
The poor little thing is waiting to be kissed ! '

In a moment the little girl was buried in
her mother's arms.

Ivan looked with infinite love at his wife,
whose face had suddenly grown crimson.
After a little while he said : ' Now, little
woman, give the child something to eat, I
believe she is famished. And after dinner
you had better get her some clothes that
she is fit to be seen in in a town . . . how
nice it will be to have something to be busy
about ! And to-morrow, or the day after,
we will go right away from Prague once more,
and get used to our little family in some
pretty hiding-place.'

THE ISLAND

BY

KAREL AND JOSEF CAPEK

ONCE upon a time there lived in Lisbon
Dom Luiz de Faria who afterwards sailed away
into the world; and when he had come to
know the greater part of it he died on the
farthest island imaginable. At the time when
he was living in Lisbon, he was a man of good
sense and of importance. He was living as
such men do live, doing well by himself and
not hindering others, and taking up as much
room as he owed to his innate pride. But
by and by even this kind of life wearied him
and became a burden, so that he turned all
his possessions into money and sailed away
in the first ship that came handy.

So they sailed first to Cadiz, then to Palermo,
Constantinople and Beirut, to Palestine and
Egypt, and round Arabia to Ceylon; then
they even sailed along the Malay Peninsula
and the island of Java, and, having regained
the open sea, they took a south-easterly course.
Sometimes they would meet with compatriots,

homeward bound, who wept with joy at hearing news of their country. In all these parts Dom Luiz saw so much that was marvellous and even seemed incredible, that he fancied he had forgotten all else. While they were sailing in the open sea, a gale overtook them, and their ship was tossed about on the waves like a cork, without direction or guidance. For three days the gale increased, and raged with unabated fury, and on the third night the ship foundered on a coral reef. Amid the most appalling noise Dom Luiz felt himself lifted high and pitched down again ; but the wave threw him back upon a raft, senseless. When he came to himself, he found that it was midday, and that he was quite alone upon the raft of splintered wood in a calm sea. At that moment he experienced the joy of living for the first time in his life. His raft kept afloat until the evening, and all through the night and throughout the next day ; but nowhere did he espy land. Moreover the spars of his raft were loosened by the water, and one piece after another dropped off. In vain did Dom Luiz try to secure them with strips of his clothing. In the end only three insecure spars were left, and he himself grew faint with weariness and the thought of his isolation. Then Dom Luiz took his leave of life and bowed himself to the will of God.

On the third day at dawn he found that the waves were carrying him to a wonderful island; it appeared to him to be rising then and there from the water with beautiful groves and green bushes. At last he was able to step on to the shore which was covered with salt and foam. At this moment some savages came out of the grove, but Dom Luiz shouted furiously at them, for he was afraid of them. Then he knelt to pray, sank down upon the ground near the shore and went to sleep.

Towards sunset hunger awoke him. The sands round about him were full of the prints of flat, naked feet, and Dom Luiz was glad to find that the savages, who were crouching round him, staring at him with wonder, and talking about him, were not doing him any harm. He went in search of nourishment, but darkness had now descended. Rounding a rock, he came upon a large number of savages, sitting in a circle and eating their supper; he saw men, women, and children in the circle, but he himself stood afar, not daring to approach, like a beggar from another parish. Then from among the others there rose up a young

native woman, and brought him fruit upon a
dish of straw. Luiz rushed upon the food,
and greedily ate the bananas, fresh and dried
figs and other fruit, meat dried in the sun,
and sweet bread of a different taste from ours.
The girl moreover brought him a pitcherful
of spring water and, crouching, watched him
as he ate. When he had eaten, his whole
body felt at ease ; he thanked the girl with a
loud voice for her gifts, for her bread and her
charity, and thanked the others for their
charity also. While he spoke, his gratitude
grew upon him like a tender constraint of
his overcharged heart, and burst forth in
words such as he had never found before.
The native woman sat opposite him and
laughed.

And Dom Luiz thought that he must repeat
what he had said, so that she should understand, and he thanked her as fervently as
though he were praying. Meanwhile all the
others had gone into the wood, and Luiz was
afraid to remain by himself with so much
joy in his heart, and in so lonely a spot. To
retain the girl, he began to tell her who he
was and whence he came, how the ship had
foundered, and what he had suffered on the
high seas. Presently Luiz noticed that she

had gone to sleep with her cheek pressed to the ground, and he got up and sat at a little distance, looked at the stars and listened to the surging of the sea, until he was overcome by sleep.

In the morning when he awoke, he looked for the woman, but she was gone ; only the imprint of her body was left in the sand at full length, straight and slender as a green branch, and when Luiz stepped into this hollow, it was warm with the sun. Then he went the round of the island by the shore, to see what it was like. Sometimes his way led him through the woods or through brushwood ; at other times he had to round a morass, or climb over a rock. Several times he met with savages, but he no longer feared them. The sea was of a blue more intense than anywhere else in the world, and the blossom-trees and plants were of a peculiar grace. He walked all day, and beheld the beauty of the most beautiful of all the islands he had ever seen. He also thought the beauty of the savages greater than that of any others. On the next day he continued his quest, until he had made the complete round of the island, which was blessed with springs and flowers, and as peaceful as we imagine the garden of Eden

to have been. At night he returned to the
spot where he had stepped ashore ; there he
found the woman sitting alone, braiding her
hair. At her feet lay the raft which had
carried him, lapped by the waves of the
impassable sea, so that he could go no further.
Dom Luiz sat down near her, and looked at
the waves which carried off his thoughts one
by one. When many hundreds of waves had
come and gone, his heart overflowed with
boundless grief. and he poured forth his
plaint : how ne had been wandering for two
days and taken the measure of all the isle,
but had nowhere found a city or harbour,
nor any man in his own likeness ; that all
his companions had perished in the sea, and
he was left alone on this island whence there
was no return, alone among savages who
spoke a language the words and meaning of
which were unintelligible to him. So he
bemoaned his fate, and the woman lay in the
sand and listened to him till she went to sleep,
lulled by the monotony of his plaint. Then
Dom Luiz ceased to speak and breathed
gently.

In the morning they sat together on a rock,
high above the sea, and looked at the horizon.
Dom Luiz thought over his whole life ; he

remembered the magnificence and preciousness
of Lisbon, his love affairs, his travels, and
everything in the world that he had seen, and
he closed his eyes, so as to find inwardly all
those beautiful pictures. But when he opened
them, he saw the woman sitting on her heels
opposite him and staring obliquely and dully
in front of her; he noticed that she was
comely with small breasts and slender limbs,
brown as reddle and very straight.

He would often sit on this rock to look for
ships. He saw the sun rise from the sea and
set therein, and he got used to this and to
everything else. He began to taste the
sweetness of this island, and it seemed to him
an isle of love. Sometimes the savages would
seek him; they held him in high esteem.
When they crouched round him they looked
like fattened geese; they were tattooed, and
some of them were very old; they brought
him food and cared for him. When the time
of the rains came, Dom Luiz went to live
in the woman's hut. Thus he lived among
the savages and was naked like them;
but he despised them and would not learn a
word of their language. He did not know
what they called the island on which he
lived, nor the roof which sheltered him, nor

the woman who was before God his sole companion.

Whenever he returned to the hut of a night, he found his supper prepared, his couch ready, and the gentle embrace of the brown woman. Although he counted her as hardly a human being, but more akin to the animals, yet he would talk to her in his own language, and was content when she listened. So he told her all the thoughts that were continually passing through his mind : of his house in Lisbon and the details of his travels. At first it annoyed him that the woman understood neither his words nor the purport of all he was telling her, but gradually he got used to this also, and told her the same things over and over again, always in the same words and manner of speech ; after that he would take her into his arms as his wife.

But in course of time his descriptions became shorter and less coherent ; many events escaped his memory as though they had never happened ; for whole days together he would lie on his couch without speaking, and think about himself. He got so accustomed to his surroundings that he would sit on the rock for hours, but never think of looking for ships.

Some years passed, and Luiz forgot his

return and his mother-tongue ; his mind was as dumb as his speech. At every nightfall he would return to his hut, but he knew no more of the woman than he had done on the first day.

One day in the summer, when he was roaming in the depth of the forest, he was suddenly seized by a great restlessness, so that he ran out into the open, and there he espied a fine ship riding at anchor. With a beating heart he ran down to the shore and mounted his rock, whence he could see a group of sailors and their officers. He hid behind a boulder like a savage and listened to their talk. Their speech touched something in his memory, and he became conscious that the strangers were talking in his own language. Then he stood up, meaning to speak to them, but he could only cry out. The strangers were startled, and he cried out for the second time. They pointed their carbines at him, and then his tongue was loosened and he called to them : ‘ Mercy, senhores ! ’ They shouted with joy and ran towards him, but, like a savage, Luiz felt that he must run away. They, however, surrounded him, embraced him one after the other, and overwhelmed him with questions. But he stood

among them naked and full of fear, anxious
to escape.

' Be not afraid,' said an old officer to him,
' remember that you are a man. Bring meat
and wine, for he looks thin and miserable.
Come and sit with us and make yourself at
home, so that you may get used to human
speech again, and not to cries which may
be the speech of monkeys.' And they gave
Dom Luiz sweet wine, preserved meat and
rusks. He sat among them as in a dream
and ate, and he felt his memory returning
to him.

The others also ate and drank, and chatted,
glad to have found a compatriot. When Luiz
had eaten, he was filled with as sweet a feeling
of gratitude as on that other day when the
woman had nourished him, and he was over-
joyed to hear his own beautiful language,
and to be with companionable human beings,
who talked to him as to a brother. The words
therefore returned readily to his tongue, and
he thanked them all as well as he could.

' Rest a little longer,' said the old officer,
' and after that you shall tell us who you are
and how you came to be here. Then the
precious gift of speech will return to you, for
man's greatest possession is that he can talk,

and communicate to others what has happened
to him and what his feelings are.'

While the officer thus spoke, a young sailor
began to sing a lovely song. He sang of a man
who sails across the sea, while his sweetheart
entreats the sea, the winds and the heavens
to send him back to her. Her longing and
sorrow were expressed in the tenderest words
imaginable. When the sailor had finished,
others sang or recited poems of a like kind,
emulating each other in sadness : they sang
of longing for the beloved one, of ships bound
for far-off countries, and of the ever-changing
sea. At last they all began to talk of their
homes and of those they had left behind.
Dom Luiz wept, happy to the verge of pain at
the thought of what he had suffered, and
that now he was able, having previously forgotten his speech, to understand again the
lovely music of poetry ; and he wept because
it was all so like a dream, and he was afraid of
the awakening.

At last the old officer got up and said :
' Boys, we will have a look at this island
which we have discovered, and we will all
return before sundown and set sail. We will
start to-night on our return journey under
God's protection. But you,' he turned to

Luiz, ' if you should possess anything in this place which you would like to take with you, as a remembrance, bring it hither and await our return at sunset.'

The sailors dispersed along the shore, and Dom Luiz turned towards the woman's hut. The nearer he drew, the more he hesitated ; he bethought himself how he could best tell her that he must go away and leave her. And he sat down on a stone by the wayside, and realized that he could not simply run away and leave her without thanking her, when he had lived with her for ten years. He remembered what she had been to him, how she had nourished him, and served him with her body and her work.   He went into her hut, sat down near her and talked hurriedly and a great deal, as though that must convince her. He told her that they had come to fetch him away, and that pressing affairs demanded that he should go ; he invented many excuses. Then he took her into his arms, thanked her for all she had done for him, and made sacred promises to return soon. When he had been talking for a long time, he became aware that she was listening without reason and understanding, and he became angry and repeated all his arguments with the greatest emphasis, and stamped his feet with impatience. Suddenly it occurred to him that the sailors might perhaps be starting without him, and he ran out in the middle of his arguments and hurried to the shore.

But as yet no one had arrived, and he sat down to wait. He began to be haunted by the thought that the woman had not properly understood what he had told her of his impending departure ; this became so unbearable that he started up and ran back, to explain it all once more to her. But when he came to the hut, instead of entering, he peered through a crack to see what she was doing. He saw that she had plucked fresh grasses and made his couch for the night of these ; that she was now preparing his meal of fruit, and he noticed for the first time that she was herself eating the inferior pieces, those which were bruised or rotting, and chose the best for him, all picked fruit, large and faultless ; then she sat down motionless like an image, and waited for him. Then Dom Luiz felt that undoubtedly he must first eat the fruit she had prepared and lie down on the couch and put an end to her waiting before he departed.

Meanwhile the sun was sinking, and the sailors were assembling on the shore, prior to their departure. None but Dom Luiz was missing, and they called him: 'Senhor! Senhor!' When he did not come, they ran to the edge of the wood, and looked and called for him there. Two of them passed quite close, calling out incessantly, but he hid in the thicket, and his heart was throbbing with fear that they might discover him. At last their calls ceased and night came on. He heard the plashing of their oars as they returned to the ship, loudly pitying the missing man. Then all was silent, and Dom Luiz crept out of the thicket and returned to the hut. He found the woman sitting motionless and patient. Dom Luiz ate the fruit, lay down on the fragrant couch and took to himself her who had been waiting for him.

Dawn rose; Dom Luiz had not been asleep; he looked out of the door of his hut towards the sea, which he could see through an opening in the trees. He saw the departing ship in the far distance. He looked at the native woman asleep by his side, and she was no longer beautiful as of yore, but hideous and terrible. Tear upon tear ran down upon her breasts while Dom Luiz repeated in whispers, so that she should not hear him, all those splendid words and wonderful poems, describing the pain of longing and ever unfulfilled desires.

Then the ship disappeared below the horizon. Dom Luiz remained on the island. But from that day, and during all the years he yet had to live, he never spoke a single word.

THE LIVING FLAME

BY

KAREL AND JOSEF ČAPEK

A CERTAIN Manoel M. L. had lived the greater part of his youth in a Southern seaport. He seemed to lack nothing that could make him happy; he enjoyed everything which his youth and his native town offered to him, was respected by men and loved by women, and by his friends also; and every one who knew him thought him a lucky man. But he himself often thought that something was wanting; that his happiness was not real; something of weariness and a dead weight was mingled therein, and this oppressed his mind with melancholy. Perhaps he was dissatisfied with himself for living as he did, instead of living a life which he was not able clearly to imagine. . . . Probably the reason was that he was living in a place where the inhabitants breathe the golden dust of far-off countries, and look out on the blue ocean which stirs all their longings, and where with a single step they can tear themselves away and sail to wherever they like. Perhaps Manoel was not distinctly conscious of all this, but only felt a secret restlessness and general longing of which he did not know whence it came or how to satisfy it.

One evening he went out to walk through the streets of his native town. Darkness had gathered, and Manoel went alone and without a set purpose; he walked until he came to the harbour, where he stood still on the quay.

The water was plashing gently, and a cool breeze was blowing from the sea. Large ships with their sails furled were bobbing up and down, and rubbing their flanks together with a crunching sound. In the centre rode a ship larger than the others, and boats with twinkling lights were dancing round it.

The thought suddenly occurred to Manoel: 'How would it be if I were to take sail for India ? '

He stood looking at the dark water and black ships. . . . 'Supposing I took sail for India ? ' he repeated. At that moment he was joined by two men; one was of a fantastically great stature, the other was black.

' Sir,' said the large one, ' have you ever known a swallow or a kite to fly as far as man with the help of God will sail ? The world, sir, consists or is composed of distances and directions. Your wife, your neighbours and your house are an annoyance to you, you are weary of your good fortune, and disappointed in your life; but in strange countries you will have neither wife nor neighbour nor house. You will be living between the four points of the compass, and every direction is open, like a high road, waiting to be taken by you. Therefore leave your prison, O man, and lock the door behind you; you will then understand and praise the exquisite wisdom which created so many directions and such great distances, proving the true might and miraculous power of God. Amen.'

'At the end of every direction,' said the negro, 'there are peoples or islands superior to everything else. Somewhere in the world you will find such wonderful things that you would fain forget all that you have known; and yet somewhere else there are still more beautiful things; you will never come to the end of them.'

'There are moreover cases,' said the large one, 'of people who settle in those strange parts, where they become governors or despots, grow immensely rich, and enjoy every woman in the country or island. Some parts also are uninhabited by either man or beast; nothing exists there but God's freedom. Yet man's real freedom is not to be found in one place, but in the whole world.'

While they were talking, they had their eyes perpetually on the ship which was making ready with unfurling sails like a bird which opens its wings to prepare for flight. A bell rang loud and long. Then the two men grudgingly stepped into their boat and begged Manoel: ' Commend us to the protection of God, noble sir.'

' Where are you going ? ' asked Manoel.

' To hell, noble sir,' said the white man, pushing off the boat with his foot.

' To both the Indies,' said the black one.

' Supposing I came with you ? ' cried Manoel and jumped into the middle of the boat. It rocked violently; the negro rowed with powerful strokes, and they struck against the flank of the large craft. They were no sooner on board than she moved off and out into the open sea.

It was thus that Manoel became a sailor for the rest of his life.

They took their course along the coast of Tunis, Egypt, Arabia and both the Indies; but Manoel did not sojourn long in any place, and when the ship returned to Europe, he went aboard another and sailed off again. The seasons and years went by, but he did not return home. He survived the foundering of several ships, the death of many companions; he recovered from malaria and other fevers, and from poisoning through swamps and insects; he received wounds which were healing while his countrymen gave him up for dead. But nowhere did Manoel find rest or lasting content; he settled nowhere, but preferred to make a miserable livelihood out of roaming land and seas. His errant life never gave him what he was hungering for, and his passion drove him on and on, until he was old and worn out with the hardships of his toil, and unable to withstand death any longer. Because he was poor, and no one asks a tramp any questions or takes him in, Manoel lay down in the road to die. But it was not ordained that he should die like the beasts of the field, nor like the ordinary man, for he was taken to the Hospital of the Brothers of Mercy. There he was put in a large ward, and above his head were written his name and the name of the illness of which he was destined to die. His hands were folded across his chest, and he was asleep.

When he awoke, a young Brother came to his bedside and said : ' Sir, a man who is dangerously ill does not know what may befall him, but even for those who are in health it is better to confess themselves and cleanse their souls of all that troubles them. Will you repent and confess, and refresh your soul with the sweet solace of redemption ? '

' I will,' said Manoel, ' for I have ever gladly tasted of all refreshments and sweetnesses which it fell to my lot to enjoy.'

Then the pious Brother hurried off to his Superior, who was a famous confessor, and told him that there was a man lying ill in the hospital who bore the character of being a heathen, and that he might now perhaps be converted and brought to confess and repent.

And the priest went to Manoel and addressed him kindly : ' My dear son, I have been told that your hours are numbered, and you are willing to pour out your soul before God and give Him an account of your deeds.' He further talked eloquently of confession, and that it was well for us to look at life as a whole before leaving it, and recapitulate our deeds, so that Manoel began truly to long to confess himself, and begged the priest to give ear to him.

' Weigh your deeds well,' said the priest,
' and remember all. Is your illness no hin-
drance to you, and are you sufficiently in your
senses not to forget important things ? '

' Never have I seen my life more clearly
and completely than at this moment,' said
Manoel.

The confessor was glad to find so much
humility in him, bade the others leave the
room and sat down at his bedside to listen.
Manoel asked : ' In what order shall I confess,
according to times, places, or my actions ? '

' As it comes most easily to you,' said the
priest, ' but I should prefer the actions. I
see you are a sensible man, and I approve your
submission to God's will. Happy is he who
takes leave of life without fear and without
reproaches, when he is about to start for the
great journey into a better world.'

' My life,' replied Manoel, ' has been full of
labour, therefore I am looking forward to a
long rest and sleep, and I do not dread the
grave, for it will be a bed without mosquitoes ;
nor the darkness, for it hides neither thieves
nor snakes. Nevermore shall I live on the
enchanting islands I have seen, nor hear the
lovely songs I have heard ; but I shall sleep,
and dream of what I have loved, and I shall

forget nothing, not one of the things I have seen.'

Manoel sat up in his bed and continued: ' There are so many experiences, and the story of my life is so long that I do not know where to begin, or how I can manage to omit nothing that is important. And how could I ever describe the beauty of all I have seen and felt? Surely, man is just to his life when he is about to die, and at this moment all my deeds and experiences seem to me of equally great importance and consequence. It was important that I left my native town, and it was important that I never returned to it, but remained in strange lands ; that I was drawn on and on, and that the desire for roaming never and nowhere left me. How could I tell you all that has happened to me ? I know every part of the world, all the islands and continents, and all the peoples inhabiting them. I need only shut my eyes, and my mind is filled with visions of which you will never be able to imagine the like ; all the songs of this world, all the dances and kisses ; all the characteristic towns, curious groves and blossoms, and all the other things of which the world is made up. I should like to celebrate all the women of different countries,

praising them according to their colour, their
bodies and dresses, all that differentiates
them and all that they have in common. I
have experienced most of the sicknesses which
different climates generate, and I have often
been a prisoner and have escaped; but even
when I was not a captive, even though I might
be resting beneath palm trees in the most
lovely parts of the world, my only longing
and desire was to escape and go yet farther
afield, so that I flew to fresh distances.'

'Sailor,' said the priest, 'I do not ask what
you have been and what you have seen, but
what deeds you have done, and what there
was of good and bad in your roaming life.'

'My deeds,' said Manoel, 'were various,
according to the various countries in which
I sojourned, but I am certain that I have
done everything which I had occasion to do.
Sometimes I was so rich that I did not know
the extent of my fortune, and sometimes I
was naked, and did not possess so much as a
stick to drive away snakes and the wicked
monkeys. At other times, it is true, I used
my stick on the obstinate backs of slaves,
and I would lean upon them, when all the
people bowed before me in the bazaars and
in the streets. But for much the greatest

part of my life I myself have served others, and carried loads like a camel.'

'All that,' the priest said impatiently, 'is no doubt very interesting, but now God is bidding you to confess your grosser sins, such as murder, violence, rape or theft, also immorality, debauchery, lying and cheating; also gambling and swearing, hurting the undefended; godlessness, want of faith. Confess not only your sinful actions, but also where you have sinned in words and thoughts against the law and against virtue.'

'No doubt I have committed deeds of that description too,' said Manoel, 'and if it is so very important that you should know, I will tell you that I have killed both in defence and also in offence, after all the rules of the game, and with much skill. If you ask me about immorality, I could describe to you the many different women I have met. Each one was like a fresh landscape, or an undiscovered island on which you set foot in wonder and curiosity. Those are details: in themselves worth telling and strange enough, but at this moment they do not seem important to me. I am wondering much more, and pondering upon it, that though the thought of the distances I was going to traverse made me shudder because they were so great, yet I joyfully and unhesitatingly threw myself into them as into an abyss.'

The priest sighed and said : ' You would do better to repent of your sins, and be forgiven by God before you go to be judged.'

But Manoel answered : ' I repent nothing that I have done. My life has been one single purpose, and what there was of good or bad beside that, I do not know. I think it was of great consequence that I should have gone in every direction of this world and sailed to every quarter, and on my way seen all the oceans and continents. Is it not of the greatest importance that I should have known so many blessed and so many unblessed places, and discovered ever fresh wonders and deeps ? '

' Fear the Last Judgement,' cried the priest loudly and angrily.

' It would be just and meet,' said Manoel, ' to apply to my life not the judgement of what is good or bad, but of how great have been the distances I have traversed. But now, alas ! I am lying on my beam-ends like a ship that has foundered, and can roam no further.'

' Go to hell, then, pig of a sailor,' cried the priest, ' I have never seen a man so stubborn

in his last hour ; a terrible curse must be
upon you that you can speak thus.'

So saying he hurried away.

' Go, priest,' Manoel called after him, ' I
do not understand what you want of me.'

The priest had gone, and Manoel turned
towards the wall to sleep. He dreamt he was
walking through the streets of a town without
knowing why or whither, until he was surprised
to find himself standing by the water's edge
of a harbour. The water was dark, gently
plashing against the flanks of black ships
which seemed abandoned, with the exception
of the one in the centre, from the deck of
which lights were glimmering, and boats were
dancing around it. Two men were standing
close to him ; they were whispering to each
other ; but Manoel tried in vain to remember
who they were, nor could he catch a single
word of their conversation, although they were
speaking his own language. While they were
talking, a powerful bell began to ring from the
ship; it was clamorous and persistent. Then
the two men got into a boat reluctantly,
and hesitating as they went. Manoel asked :
' Where are you going ? '

One of them said distinctly, so that Manoel
understood : ' To hell.'

' Supposing I went with you ! ' cried Manoel, seized by a passionate desire, and jumped into the middle of the boat.

The boat drew near to the ship, water and darkness melted into one, and Manoel himself was drawn into the unreality and phantasmagoria.

The Brother who was sitting by his bedside had been sure for some little time that Manoel was dead : he prayed over him.

Then he went off to fetch water to wash him, and a shroud.

AT THE ROTARY MACHINE

BY

K. M. ČAPEK-CHOD

BEFORE the eyes of Kuba, whose nickname was ' Spattered Kuba,' a strip of paper, about two yards in width, was madly careering down with a speed which the chance onlooker would have found it difficult to estimate. It unwound itself from an immensely fat spool, which was so heavy that it took the full strength of two workmen to lever it into the position where it turned ; this spooled the strip into the unwieldy, polished printing machine, which first of all directed it into a narrow reservoir where it was moistened by a scarcely perceptible vapour ; then it was squeezed between two cylinders, one of which was smooth, while the other was covered with a surface of cast metal consisting of thousands of letters, so that one turn of the cylinders printed eight pages of a newspaper. The interminable strip flew on to a second pair of cylinders which supplied it with another eight pages on the reverse side, wherewith the first two sheets of the number were finished. But the strip continued on its mad career, twisting itself through a whole labyrinth of cylinders, which printed further pages on further sheets; through sharp, tiny wheels which indented, through knives which cut it across : through disks which touched it with sticking-paste : through steel arms which folded it, till it reached the point where it was met by another strip of half its size, which had undergone the same treatment of cylinders, disks, knives and arms, and had thereby been turned into a supplement. By an ingenious device this was folded and pasted into the number, so that both paper streams, ready printed, cut and pasted, emerged from the opening as the complete newspaper, of which five copies a second were deposited on a stand, and taken off by the hands of young transport workers.

All this happens amid an overpowering, penetrating din, as though a gale were shrieking with inharmonious howls through the pipes of a gigantic organ, or as if all the two hundred thousand readers of the daily paper, collected under the vault of the printing house, were reading all the columns at the same time in breathless haste. Every word that is spoken is swallowed up by the noise ; the men communicate with each other by signs only, or they put their mouth close to their companion's ear and shout into it with the full power of their lungs.

But there is no time for unnecessary talk. The Sunday Paper is being printed in two editions, and every second of lost time costs five copies. From the moment when the overseer takes the seal off the indicator which gives the number of copies, every workman becomes a part of the machinery which has to perform certain movements within a certain time. From eleven at night till four in the morning, during the five hours while printing is going on, under stress of perpetual excitement, in the heat of an oven, none of the slaves of this despotic metal monster is conscious of himself. Their eyes anxiously watch the course of the shiny white paper, which is lit up by electric lamps at points of danger, and their hands are upon the levers to stop the machine instantly, should the paper get torn, which may happen at any moment through too much moistening or through a tiny pleat.

On the stopping of the machine at the right moment depends the immensely valuable economy of time, and the smooth working of a new installation for inserting a fresh roll of paper by machinery.

Otherwise the machine is never stopped before a roll, measuring several thousands of yards, comes to an end on one side or the other; then a fresh one has to be mounted. A whole row of them can be seen through the door which opens into the courtyard. They will all be required to-day.

When a fresh roll is needed, or there is another urgent reason, any one of the workmen may stop the clanking colossus; no one, however, except one of the two chief engineers is allowed to let down the machinery, for it is necessary to get inside it to set the lathes which carry the paper on its entire course, or to rectify the torn strip of paper; and there is not the slightest doubt that this immense mechanism would grind human bones as easily as produce a newspaper.

There are three levers by means of which the machine can be stopped, one at each of the cylinders, and one at the opening for the passage of the printed copies. Spattered Kuba is in charge of one of these levers, and is responsible for stopping the machine the moment he notices a tear or pleat in the unwinding paper.

Spattered Kuba is at this moment staring at the snow-white surface, watching its tension and moistness, which he has to estimate. His hand reaches out now for the brass wheel of the brake, now for the handle of the lever. It is his duty at the same time to watch the glass tubes of the oil reservoirs which grease the axles of the wheels that are in his charge ; overheating or firing would mean an accident, or else the end of the world . . . that is, the non-appearance of the paper on the following morning !

A noise as of thunder is roaring beneath the vault of the printing-house ; the brass axles of the innumerable cylinders which grind the print turn in their steel beds, from which drops of oil are oozing ; through the fine dust which rises from the crushed paper, electric lamps are shining with a steady glow. Spattered Kuba has eyes for nothing but his paper, his axles and taps.

He seems to have no thought but for this. His tall, bony figure, covered with a blue blouse which is tucked into his trousers so that there should be no fulness in which a tooth of the machinery could catch, is standing upright like a statue ; only the thin bare arms are moving : they have hard broad muscles,

and sinews like the strings of a double bass.
The right hand ever hovers near the lever.
His arms are covered with black, oily smears;
drops of sweat are on his forehead and run
down his cheeks in rivulets. Perhaps it is
for this reason that his companions have
called him 'spattered' Kuba, or it may be
because of the freckles with which his plain,
red-bearded face is sprinkled; they are as
large as a threepenny piece.

His absorption in his work is, however, only
apparent. His thoughts are flying, perhaps
not as fast as the mad paper-strip in front of
him, yet in the course of the two hours since
he has been standing there, he has been totting
them up one by one, and the sum-total which
he has drawn in the end is so fearful that
it scares him; but not a single movement
betrays what he is thinking.

The sum-total is that he is going to kill
somebody to-night. He can see his victim
every time he looks up. The head, covered
with a silk skull-cap, is just visible between
the framework and the cylinder, bending now
over the indicator, now over the tablet on
which he enters the number of copies which
have passed through. He is the overseer in
charge, and Kuba is going to kill him to-night.

That is an absolute certainty ; he wishes everything else were as firmly settled as that.

There is the place where he will be drenched in his own blood ; where he will bleed to death like an ox, there, inside the machine, with just room enough underneath the cylinders for a man to crouch and insert the paper by the light of an electric lamp.

Kuba has seen it done once when he was working at a cotton printer's, and knows what the power of these cylinders is when they are at work.

Cotton had been printed in this manner long before it had occurred to any one that newspapers might be produced in the same way. One of the workmen there had let the cylinders down on an overseer who had worried him ; it had torn off his arm ' as though it had been a travelling bag,' and the machine had gone on as though nothing had happened.

Spattered Kuba can do it when he likes, at any of the shifts of paper rolls ; he will have time to do it until four o'clock in the morning ; any one of the white rolls with which the yard is filled may bring death to the tyrant.

It is going to happen in exactly an hour's time, and death is approaching in the shape of the fourth roll, which has a torn cover ; it will soon be rolled into the workshop. The three preceding ones are standing in front of it like hour-glasses ; their turn will come, will surely come, and after that—death.

The heat in the printing-house increased with every puff of the vaporizer which moistens the paper ; Kuba felt a rivulet of perspiration running down his shoulder-blades. But whenever he bent his head forward a stream of icy cold October air from outside struck his temples ; his head was reeling with a fit of appalling toothache, and mad fury shook his whole fame.

This accursed, hellish pain had been the cause of all his troubles ! Every night, as soon as he had taken his stand at the machine, it had seized upon him, and held his head as in a vice. Just a fortnight ago, on a night like this, Kuba had tried a remedy that some one had recommended, he did not remember who : ' Drink half a pint of brandy in one draught, and in two twinks the pain will leave you . . . absolutely dead gone.'

He had never drunk brandy as long as he lived, but on that occasion he did. The pain really had left him, but when the overseer had passed him on his round, he had stopped, although Kuba had done his utmost to hold his breath. ' What, you drink brandy ? ' he had said, ' then we have no use for you here at night ; come for your discharge in a fortnight.'

The overseer had said it like everything else he said, short and sharp like a cut with a whip. Kuba knew that all remonstrance would be useless. He said nothing all that fortnight, but his wrath grew within him.

He had been looking everywhere for work. ' My dear fellow, you are none too young,' or ' Do you think we keep our workmen for the benefit of the panel doctor ? ' were the answers in the printing houses where they worked with steam.

Yesterday the manager of a factory had sent him away with the advice to apply for work as a scavenger. And he was only forty-seven ! That had been as if some one had struck him in the face with his fist. It had happened in the suburb of Lieben, and all the afternoon he had wandered about at the back of the Karoline Valley. When he had returned home to Ziskov, his family had increased by two ; his wife had been prematurely confined and presented him with twins. When there were six already ! That was no small matter.

Then at last his bitterness had given way for a moment. Who knows but what God had sent him these two little angels to help him ? If he were to tell the overseer of this increase in his family, and two at once. That must move his heart, even if it were made of stone. Otherwise he would not have said a word, but now that the twins had come. . . . He wished he had bitten off his tongue rather ! Evidently his words had gone home and touched the overseer, but all the same he had shrugged his shoulders : ' he had no use for a drunkard who might do harm, kill somebody or endanger the issue of the newspaper. And so far as he was concerned, Kuba might have triplets.'

After these two long weeks his stubborn fury had for the first time given way to sorrow on this last night at his work, while he was cleaning his machinery until it looked like the inside of a watch seen through a magnifying glass. For the last time ! And yet he had always seen single-handed to this part of the work, and never failed in one of his duties.

But when the machinery had started, and began to roar with a thousand wild sounds, his sorrow vanished, and when the stream of paper was flowing past him, illuminated by an oblique, dazzling light, it made him feel giddy for the first time.   Then when the icy draught struck his temples again and he felt that boring pain in his jaws, his strength left him, and a hard, mad fury took its place such as he had never felt in all his life.   What he had turned over in his mind for the last two hours had now become an unalterable resolve : ' If I am here for the last time, he is ! '

When this terrible thought had first occurred to him, he had rejected it with the comment : ' It would serve him right ! '   But it returned again and again ; it rode upon his neck like a demon which would not be shaken off.   It was as if every sharp stab of pain in his temples spurred him on to it.

From out the tumult of vociferous metallic noises which struck the vault with endless shrieks from throats neither knowing nor needing respite, there seemed to come to him the crying of his infants, the twins.   It went on without ceasing, worrying him with its monotony, and at times he imagined he could see the two little heads reflected on the interminable white strip, as he had seen them on the white pillow before he left his home.   He

saw the two wide-open mouths and the tiny
quivering nostrils quite distinctly. And he
saw the eyes of his wife into which he had not
dared to look all this fortnight ; they had
pursued him from the corner of the room
behind the door. Before he had left, she
had called him to her and said in a hardly
audible whisper : ' Jakob, you are out of
work, I know it ; Mrs Skemralka has told me
to-day . ∴ . what are we going to do . . .
for God's sake . . . Jesus Mary. . . .' And
she had begun to cry.

It was a curious thing, but as soon as the
cylinders left off turning and the engine
stopped, these visions ceased, and now, at
the moment when he ought to have done
what he wanted to do, his courage failed him,
and his reason returned. While the overseer
inside the engine was putting in the fresh
paper, two workmen were turning the machine
with a separate lever in obedience to the
orders from inside : ' Slowly . . . enough
. . . go on.' It would only have needed a
movement of Kuba's hand towards the lever,
and the overseer would never have given
another order. But Kuba became like a
statue, his arm cleaving to his body. He
wished he were at least capable of looking at

the place where the overseer was putting his fingers positively between the teeth of the beast like a tamer who may do as he likes with the lion's mouth.

But he could not even do that, and before he was able to collect himself the familiar dry sound of the rustling paper indicated that it was passing over the cylinders again, and the overseer cried : ' Stop ! ' He crept out, and a click at the cylinder indicated that the leverage had been put out of action ; the men cried : ' Ready,' and the chief engineer, in virtue of his sole right, set the machinery going again. For a second it hummed like a spindle, and then roared afresh like a water-fall. And with its voice Satan was beginning to speak again ; he laughed at Kuba's cowardice, and seared his temples as with flames. As soon as Kuba thought of his home, he heard the crying of the twins, and then his murderous desire grew in him to such an extent that he could hardly wait for the paper-roll to be finished. But when the time came, he could not move.

So it came to pass that the fourth roll, the one with the torn cover, with death riding on it, went down the maw of the machine without injuring a hair on the overseer's head ; that the seventh also passed the same way with a blot of oil on it which pursued it through all the copies, and that at last only two rolls were left.

When the last but one was hauled up, the last but one : ' Ready ! ' was called. And again spindle and waterfall were set in motion. Once more, for this last chance, the demon bestrode Kuba's soul and heated his brain with the thought : ' If I don't do it now, it will never be done.'

Although he bit his teeth together to master the unendurable pain, they chattered, and he gulped and struggled for breath from time to time. His hands and feet trembled as though he were in a fever, and when he reached out for the brake, his fingers shook violently. In all his life he had never experienced so much searing rage, such intense passion as he did now, while the moments rushed on madly, and yet too slowly for his murderous intention. At last !

They were hauling up the last roll. Kuba had to hold on to something, else he would have fallen down. If he had been commanded to stir from his place, he would have been unable to do so. He could not even turn his head and look at his victim, so as to be ready

to start the engine suddenly and let it seize
his hand at the right moment, when he had
his fingers between the cylinders.

' Slowly . . . enough . . . ' he heard him say.

Kuba started up. The red-hot vice which
seemed to have held his head round the
temples, now twisted it round by the neck,
and his smarting eyes looked at what they
had not dared to look on before, the inside
of the machine. He saw the curly head
of the overseer, saw the fingers of his
right hand, which were deftly putting the
paper between the cylinders. The moment
had come.

The spasmodic impulse which had twisted
his head round, was now tearing his arm from
his side and bringing his fist to the handle of
the lever. But what was happening ?

The white light of the electric lamps turned
to a blood-red glow, the twists of electric wire
became yellow, then red, and went out. All
this did not take more than half a second,
then there was complete darkness. Curses
and shouts were heard.

But within this half second a mad thought
rushed through Kuba's mind : Satan himself
had sent him this darkness, so as to cover the
deed and its perpetrator. Who could say

which of the three levers had set the engine
in motion ?

Quickly now, while he is inside !

A thousand sparks were dancing in a huge
circle before Kuba's eyes, while with a violent
movement he reached out for the handle
. . . he reeled, feeling a sudden sharp pain
in his right hand.

But above everything he was feeling a
supreme joy in satisfied revenge. The
machine began to puff and roar and rush like
a waterfall. Above the din Kuba fancied he
heard the screams of pain from his victim's
throat . . . he even heard words. . . .

But the roaring ceased suddenly, and turned
into mere humming. Kuba realised that this
humming was only in his ears, that the engine
was silent, and that the voice of the overseer
was going on, but not in the least in pain or
in agony.

' Damn that fellow down below, is he asleep ?
Somebody run and see what's the matter.
And no reserve light either ! Does a match
cost a fortune in this place ? '

A light was flickering, a burning match was
raised to the gas-burner, which hissed and
caught. Close to the flame Kuba saw the
face of the overseer, who had himself lighted

the gas, in sharp outline.   Three other flames shot up on the walls and lighted up the large room.

The engine had not moved.   The two other workmen were standing at their levers, waiting for further orders.   There was absolute silence, and all the eyes which had been turned on the gas-jets, returned to their work.   The hands of the transport workers could be heard banging the copies to press them down. Familiar noises were starting again.

The overseer who had crept out of the machine at the moment when the light went out, looked at the cylinders which were in working order, then he stood up, and his eyes met Kuba's look of horror.

They held him with a look so severe and fixed, that Kuba was unable to turn his eyes away.   His feet were trembling, his heart beat as though it would tear itself from the flesh.   For a good while the overseer looked him in the eyes, then suddenly his own severe eyes were lighted up by a smile so genial and almost friendly, that Kuba could not help smiling back at him.   The overseer gave him a nod which expressed trust and at the same time a warning.   Then he turned to the two other workmen.

' Attention ! ' he called out.

The brake left the cylinder with a click, the men cried : ' Ready.'

The chief engineer set the lever in motion, the engine purred like a spindle, and broke into a roar like a waterfall, to finish the last ten thousand copies. Not until much later, when the paper stream was again rushing past, did Kuba dare to look at his knuckles. He had grazed the skin of all four of them. In the darkness and unspeakable excitement he had missed the handle and dashed his hand with his full strength against a piece of metal which had taken the skin off his knuckles and made his hand bleed. His over-wrought senses and unfettered imagination, combined with the rushing of the blood in his temples, had misled him into thinking that he had really set the engine in motion under cover of darkness.

The last few hundred copies had long been sent into the neighbouring office whence came the sound of thuds with which the stamps were affixed to the postal copies. Somebody was preparing a shakedown on which to spend the night till sunrise; the printing-press, covered with paper dust, and defaced by numberless streaks of stale oil, stood still and silent, as though it were as tired as its servants. Kuba did not stir; he stared in front of him as if he had been annihilated, looking without thought or consciousness at some object which he did not take in.

The overseer, who was putting on his overcoat, came up to him: 'Well, Spattered Kuba,' he addressed him, 'if you have not found another job we will keep you on . . . what the devil has happened to your hand? I am always telling you men, you won't be careful until one of you leaves his paw in the machine. And as you have told me that you get the toothache at that lever, you can change places with Strizek; there is no draught in that place.'

And the overseer moved towards the door: 'Ah . . . haaaa . . .,' he yawned, covering his mouth with his hand.

' Sir,' stammered Kuba, crushed with shame, while the tears were rising in his eyes, 'sir, God repay you. . . .'

' Don't be a fool, old man, you know we have got to be strict. I have had to put in a good word for you with the manager. If it hadn't been for those twins . . .

well, so long.' And he shut the door behind him.

Kuba sat down on a barrel of print, pressed his face into his oil-smeared hands and sobbed, letting the tears trickle through his fingers.

THE DEATH OF
COUNT CHRISTOPHER DES LOGES

BY

F. X. ŠALDA

HE was too infirm now to walk alone ; two footmen in grey liveries, with coarse, red, clean-shaven faces, led him hither. Up till now they had accompanied rather than led him, but the doctor had pointed out to them the possibility of a fall, and this had made them be on their guard constantly ; they were therefore also constantly anxious and cross.

Only last year he had still been able to come here by himself—now and then accompanied by his doctor—to this garden of varieties which startled the casual observer like the incoherent ramblings of a lunatic's imagination. It was as if a team of whims had taken the bit between the teeth and come to grief within sight of the onlooker.

There was a clearing in the quietest and most remote part of the park, covered with

frail grasses, that were scorched by the heat
at this season. It was planted with trees;
some were tall, some undersized, some quite
stunted; some were well-matured, some of
more recent growth; some were indigenous,
while others, of exotic origin, were doing
badly in their present conditions. A few were
taken out of the hothouses when the weather
was fine, and placed by the gardeners in the
exact positions in which the aged count liked
to see them, so that close to a group of fine,
bristling Northern firs, stunted olives, oranges
and lemon trees would languish in wooden
tubs, sheltered from the north wind, and
unfold their large blossoms. Here a mimosa
drooped its long sprays over a myrtle bush,
there it would mingle its sweetness with that
of the rose of Jericho or an Ailanthus: laurels
touched Japanese camelias, and next to the
proud, funereal obelisk of a cypress, enfolded
within its severe shape like a frosty cloud
whose outlines no wind will disturb, an aspen
responded to the slightest breeze, so that it
seemed almost as if its leaves were raising the
wind of themselves.

All these trees and shrubs had been brought
hither from his travels in distant lands by
Christopher des Loges, who had been a great

adventurer, lover, and man of the world. Most
of them he had planted in this curious garden
with his own hands. They were a secret
code in which he had written down the most
interesting part of his life-story. The idea
had been suggested to him at the Vallée aux
Loups, where as a young attaché he had
visited Chateaubriand, who interested him as
a great diplomatist, not as a poet. But
Count Christopher possessed a still more
fastidious discretion. He often thought of
the distinguished old man, depressed with age,
fame, and especially with an intolerable ennui
and sterile melancholy. Chateaubriand had
taken his young colleague round the garden,
his face overshadowed with the cool cloud of a
silent pride, and had shown him with a short,
tired movement of his hand the cedars from
Lebanon and the pines from Champagne
which he had brought back from his travels.
Count Christopher never could understand
why this man had written his *Mémoires d'outre
tombe*, when he had created this singular park
for the reception of his memories. And because
of his not understanding, he showed himself
to be more of the aristocrat of the old school
than Chateaubriand himself.

Every shrub, every tree had a name ; each

one reminded the count of an event, or at least of a distinct impression or emotion; a grave, a drunken orgy, a woman, a friend; this stood for a broken vow, that for a disappointed hope, an unappreciated devotion, or unjustifiable hatred.

There was a birch, shimmering in the sun, which had been brought from the Polish plains, and named 'Mecislava.' Des Loges had plucked it from the grave of a beautiful woman for whose sake he had fought a duel, and whom he then had cast off; soon afterwards she had died. When he had visited Masovia for the second time, he had pulled the slender sapling from her snow-covered, neglected grave, on a night when he had ridden from the village inn to the castle, in company with a wild cavalcade of drunken comrades. He had made a detour to ride across the cemetery; when he returned to overtake his companions, he had very nearly lost his life. The little tree, strapped to the saddle, had startled the horse which was unaccustomed to carrying such a singular object, and had thrown the count. In the morning he was found, half frozen, and with a broken ankle.

In another part a stunted pine in a tub

reminded the aged man of her wonderful mature sisters, under whose umbrella-shaped crowns he had been wont to lay down the languid body of his Roman mistress on a bed of copper-coloured wild lilies and tenderest anemone leaves. All that his endless cruises along the coast and melancholy drives through the Campagna had meant to him, was enshrined in this insignificant little tree.

Far back, at the end of the plantation, a larch bristled with clumps of delicate needles. Thirty years ago it had been a tiny tree in a clearing, and had marked Christopher's place in a duel with a famous swordsman. He had thought it unlikely on that occasion that he would return alive. But the Sempervivum, a blossom that possesses magic charms, being the plant of immortality, was growing around him thickly from the crevices of the crumbling terrace; the herb of the blue-green god, brought hither from Greece.

Then there were trees and shrubs at which Count Christopher hardly dared to look; at least he always took off his eyes as soon as they fell on them, as though they had been scorched with glowing coals. Some memories one carefully avoids, perhaps for the very reason that it is no longer necessary to do so.

288 H³

Daily during the summer, when the weather was fine, Count Christopher des Loges, great adventurer, lover, and man of the world, and now a weak-minded septuagenarian, was led hither, tottering and supported by the two lackeys with dull red faces and a vague brutal fury hidden deep down under their clean-shaven skin and mask-like faces. There were moments when the count's eyes rested scruti-nizingly on these faces, and the old man seemed to grind something between his teeth. To be able to fasten your nails into these masks! Could they be torn off? Much blood would no doubt gush forth. Beasts! It seemed to him as if all life had crept far down below the surface, underneath its bark, or had hidden itself behind a mask. Here then he would sit, handsome and proud even in his decay, on a deck-chair brought by one of the footmen. There was still something leonine about his head with its grey locks and promi-nent cheek bones, with the sensual, disdainfully curved lips and forbidding expression. As he sat there, his head bent forward, his hands resting on the knob of his stick, he seemed more like an injured man brooding on revenge than one crushed by age. His heavy eyelids only, half covering his eyes and raised with difficulty, and the deep lines across his cheeks betokened his decay.

During the days of this summer, as soon as he had sunk back into his chair and told the lackeys to be off, he would lose himself in silent, passionate dreams. He was living through his youth once more. The more recent layers of his memory had died already, had decayed, and disclosed the older strata. Events and pictures long obliterated began to glow and spend their last warmth on the aged man when he sat in the heat of the midday summer sun, which made the sluggish blood course more violently through his veins. His lips meanwhile remained cold and half-open, like those of a man dying of thirst; his throat felt dry, and his dull eyes glowed as in a fever.

Sometimes he would ask the lackeys who came to fetch him to his dinner: ' Has Lisa come ? And do not forget, the Haydn Quartet are coming to-night.'

But Lisa had been rotting for a score of years in the chapel vault, and the players of the Haydn Quartet had been dispersed even longer than that, and fate had blown them hither and thither before throwing their bones into the cemeteries of various countries.

' Very good, Your Honour,' the lackeys would answer by the doctor's orders, and wink at each other.

There was one thing in real life which could still excite the aged count : the naked feet of women, of the labouring women who worked in the plantations, and were sometimes obliged to pass him on their way. His eyes under the once arched brows would open wide, and from under his eyelids a flash dart forth which greedily devoured the foot from the sole upwards, and rested on the hips, excitedly but with the critical appraisement of the connoisseur.

On this August day when the air was trembling with heat, and fire was pouring down from the sky, the count was sitting in his deck-chair as usual. He had taken his wonted walk through the bizarre plantation, but to-day he had tarried longer over it. He had stood still in places which he avoided as a rule, from which he would purposely turn away. For a long time he had stood looking at a small tree in a round wooden tub which the gardener had just carried out from the hothouse ; it was a Taggiasca, the rarest kind of olive, which covers the steep hillsides of Porto Mauricio on the Italian Riviera. He had gazed at the pruned tree for a long time, then uttered a senile groan and shuffled towards his chair.

Under the influence of the sun's hot rays he remembered steep terraces covered with olive trees, wonderful olive trees, hundreds of years old, peopled with wood sprites ; eloquent as a grave ; personal in their individuality, like great men. He remembered olive-mills driven by rushing waters amid moss and ferns, and hands of women working among these terraces generation after generation. He thought of a pair of particularly small hands, passionate in their embraces, and ever ready to snatch up a knife, and of white, sinuous and affectionate feet which he had pursued in their flight up those terraces that seemed to be made for chamois' feet. Then he saw those same feet, white, sinuous and affectionate, dashed against the rocks ; saw the black rocks spattered with hot blood spilled through his fault. . . .

Again the aged man groaned ; it was a sound so hollow and horrible that he was startled himself for a moment, as if he thought that not he but some one else had uttered it. He did not know how long he had been sitting there ; his thoughts were concentrated on

one tragic point. He could see nothing but
those white, sinuous, affectionate feet that had
been destroyed through his fault. He saw
them running over the rocks, or moving in a
graceful dance ; he saw them stark and dead,
showing almost severe and threatening from
under the mist of the light covering. The
sun madly beat down upon the earth, the
crickets chirped their metallic, deafening song,
the blood in his temples was throbbing, but
all these sounds melted into one, and the aged,
embittered man heard only the sound of waves
dashing against rocks that were spattered
with blood which he had wantonly wasted.

The laughter of a young thing, apparently
approaching him, suddenly startled him from
his dream. At the same time he saw a pair
of graceful, light, sinuous and gentle feet,
which together with the laugh produced an
effect of something musical and irresponsible.
An intoxication as from the aroma of a fine
hock rose to the count's head and deceived
him with a mad anticipation.

A number of young women and girls ran
past him with their skirts tucked up high ;
some were carrying rakes on their shoulders.
About a dozen naked feet danced and floated
past him, but only one pair belonged to *her* ;

he would have known them among a thousand.

All his senses were roused. His eyes dilated with a magnificent, primeval wildness, his veins swelled, and his whole body showed a single tragic pose, the hunger for the fulfilment of passion, or death. It was as if his youth, long since dead, had been allowed to return once more, to give this weak body a mad, deadly tension, while the final blow was held suspended above his head.

The girls, horrified at this sight, were seized with animal fear, and fled in wild confusion as from a catastrophe.

' Rita ! Rita ! ' The aged man's groan seemed to issue not from his throat only but from his whole body. A frightened girl ran down the steep incline, the count pursued her. This chase after youth did not last long ; it soon turned into a chase after death. Count Christopher of a sudden stumbled over the stump of a tree and fell heavily, knocking his temple against one of the boulders which were lying about in this part of the grounds. He fell without a sound.

' Look at the monster . . . so old and so sinful ! ' said one of the footmen, who had been called by the girls.

'What do you expect? A good horse will die in harness,' said the other and grinned. He did not know that he had summed up Count Christopher's philosophy in these words.

They lifted him up and carried him to the castle with the lazy steps of footmen. He was heavy, and they often stood still, mopped their faces and yawned.

THE NAUGHTY CHILD

BY

OTOKAR THEER

IF the learned counsel permits, I should like to thank him for his brilliant defence, which in spite of its thoroughness and ability has resulted in my condemnation. I am saying this without bitterness or irony ; I know only too well that in the eyes of the majority of people my case is one that deserves no pity.

I am not asking for it either. But before I die, I should like to say a few words which may subsequently help psychologists in the analysis of a certain type to which I belong. This is my case :

I am the fifth and youngest child of a customs officer·in a small provincial town. There were three sisters and a brother older than myself. My father, who had been annoyed at the birth of three daughters successively, is said to have been mad with joy at the arrival of this my elder brother. But this happiness did not last long, for the boy was sickly all

225

through his infancy, and every winter his life hung in the balance.

All his hopes, therefore were centred in me. I was the first child in the town known to have a perambulator with rubber wheels, a fact on which the entire population commented for years afterwards. I was dressed up like a doll, and decked out in ribbons. When the nurse carried me out, I was wrapped in a red shawl shot with gold. People turned round to look after me, and the great lady of the place, the countess, once left her carriage in the market square in view of everybody, to kiss my forehead.

Imagine my father's happiness, sir ! He was of humble birth. Through a happy combination of circumstances he had been able to take his degree at a university, and to marry a comparatively rich wife. Being an ambitious man, he looked upon every member of his family as a means to attain the social success for which he was longing. Unfortunately my brother and sisters took after my mother, who was a plain little woman with a nose like a knob ; they had also inherited her homeliness and slow peasant mentality.

So my father looked upon me as the sole hope of the family. I soon enjoyed endless

privileges : I was free to beat the nurse and
use my youngest sister as a riding-horse. My
fair hair was allowed to grow and was twisted
into curls. With my bright blue eyes and
a lace collar I was not unlike the princes
in van Dyck's picture. I had no difficulty in
wiping out the remembrance of naughty tricks
by engaging looks and rippling laughter.

The sum of my little sins increased. Once
I devastated a pansy-bed and did not leave
one plant alive ; another time I threw a stone
at the gardener's boy and hurt his head. One
day I nearly set the house on fire by a shot
from a toy gun which I fired close to the
curtains.   As a rule allowances were made
for me ; only now and then, when things
became too bad, my father would make his
displeasure felt. But then I used to sulk,
and as every one was silent when I would not
speak, my father generally capitulated very
soon. He would pet me and give me a penny.
At this price I consented to be conciliated,
for I was passionately fond of snow-cakes of
which fifteen could be bought for a penny.

I was sent to school before I was ten. The
masters were astonished at my precocity. But
I did not like going to school. The close air
of the school-rooms did not suit me, and I

grew thin, and complained of headaches. As I was treated differently from the other children, my complaints resulted in my going to school only now and then on visits. I thought my fellow-pupils coarse and rude ; they jeered at me, examined and felt me all over, and made me feel like a man who has fallen among a herd of monkeys. They drank up my little bottle of wine which the doctor had prescribed for my anæmia, pulled my sandwiches out of my pocket, and ate the chocolate with which my mother provided me. I went home crying.

At last my parents decided to take me away from school altogether. For whole days I played in the nursery, and my laughter once more rang through the house.

Then I was sent to the High School. Favouritism continued to shelter me ; I was not forced to work, and spent most of the school hours in playing tric-trac under the desk with my neighbour. My masters unanimously declared that I was a genius, but lacked application.

When I was thirteen, my father was given an appointment in Prague. This change in my surroundings was the first rung on the ladder of those misfortunes to which fate has chained me ever since. In the country our circumstances had placed me among the well-to-do ; now we had arrived in an inferno of noisy streets, and women in expensive dresses. My father, instead of being one of the influential people, had become merely one of a thousand civil servants.

The masters, who were apt to take for granted that a pupil from the provinces must be badly taught, worried me like devils. They treated me as though I were either an idiot, or else a dangerous ne'er-do-weel. Far from being a favourite myself, I saw others being favoured. I once ventured to give my opinion on this point to our Latin professor, a dried-up little man with a badger's face, who enjoyed nothing more than giving bad marks.

From that day onward school-life became a torture-chamber, with the masters as executioners. I became neurotic ; at one moment I would burst into tears, at the next go mad with fury. I fought sanguinary battles with my more favoured comrades.

The final result at the examination was that I failed in five subjects. This had the effect of changing the feelings of my parents towards me. My elder brother, a conscientious

worker, who until recently had been regarded
as a bundle of stupidity at home, earned
decent   reports   through   sheer   industry,
while I, ' the prodigy,' was left behind. When
my brother was moved into the upper form,
my father gave him a cigar on Sundays as an
outward sign of his new dignity. I hated him
for this cigar ; I hated him for having usurped
my place in the home ; hated him for having
to wear out his clothes ; hated him as I hated
my masters and fellow pupils.

A cousin in the cadet corps became my
ideal. I used to visit him at the barracks in
Joseph Square, and listened rapturously to
the cracking of rifles, the rhythmic steps of
the drilling soldiers, the drums, and the
pleasant chatting when the command ' Stand
easy ' had been given. We smoked cigars
and drank wine together in the canteen ; for
the first time in my life I listened to talk about
women, and it drifted into my soul like sparks.
I already fancied myself dressed in a blue
uniform with bright buttons, wearing the
white gloves that caress a woman's cheek
so pleasantly.

It was proposed, then, that I should enter
the cadet-corps. I had to undergo a physical
examination, and the medical officer declared

me unfit for military service on account of a congenital weakness. I ran out of the room; in the passage I burst into tears; I wept as though my heart were breaking. I could have beaten my father and mother who had made me a cripple at birth.

Work seemed to me more useless than ever. I argued that if my parents were responsible for my being born a cripple, it was also their duty to make up to me for the happiness which had slipped through my fingers. I was quite clear on this point, that they were under obligation to me, not I to them.

But far from honouring these obligations, my father apprenticed me to a bricklayer, after I had firmly refused to re-enter the torture-chamber of the school.

It so happened that my master put me to work at a new house which was being built close to the barracks of the cadet corps. My imagination was busy all the time with drilling, fixing bayonets, and attacking the enemy with my companies. And here I was, having to hand bricks, and fetch tobacco for a drunken foreman. I had thoughts of jumping into the Moldavia.

At last my parents realized that this state of things was unbearable. They took me away from the bricklayer, and from that time onwards my life became an Odyssey. I was clerk to an income-tax collector in a provincial town ; assistant to a chemist ; I worked in a brewery. I waded through oceans of malt, pounded drugs, listened to the chink of money on the collector's table. Sometimes I stuck to my job for two months, sometimes for a fortnight. I was unsuccessful in everything, on account of my ineradicable repugnance to work, which was the foundation of my character.

My father, not knowing what to do with me, threatened me with a house of correction. I was spared this humiliation only because my mother, when she heard of it, had a heart attack which very nearly cost her her life.

I was now twenty-one. I loitered about the streets of Prague all day long in shabby clothes and greasy collars. The continual noise of the traffic, the lighted shop windows with their glittering display, all these things were to me what the smell of food is to the starving. With my hands in my pockets, feverishly trying to find a single coin in them, I stood on the pavements, watching the ebb and flow of passers-by. I saw women with magnificent busts, shown to the best advantage by enormous lace fichus ; women with tiny hands, and small black boots which I could have kissed ; this endless procession of fragrant femininity passed me, and vanished without deigning to give me a single glance. This would drive me almost mad at times. My senses became confused, and I fancied I could hear in the clatter of the horses' hoofs the chink of the money for which I might have bought any one of these charming, elegant creatures.

How I ached for these women ! But what do you, sir, know about that ? You have had enough money to buy mistresses, and when you were tired of them you got married, and are now smoking your cigars in the family circle, surrounded by your children.

The irritability of my nerves grew worse when I became acquainted with others who were as unhappy and disappointed as I was. We met daily. Debates were our sole occupation. We debated in reeking top-floors in the room of one or the other of us ; we debated on endless promenades along the embankment ; in cafés that were open all night ; we debated over empty cups of coffee finished hours ago.

Sometimes we all burst out crying and embraced each other, as though we were on the point of taking a leap into an abyss.

I began to read sociological literature, certain books in red covers, the very titles of which would make a bourgeois like you, sir, shiver. I tried to find an explanation in these books for the reason why I should be starved of all the good things which others enjoyed. But I sought in vain.

These are the reasons, and they are the sole reasons, sir, why I fired the three shots at the fat bourgeois, the first man who on a certain day crossed my path. I had no personal grievance against him, and if it had been you, instead of now being my brilliant defender, you would have been my victim. To me this bourgeois was simply symbolical of a certain class which does no more work than I did, and yet is rich and happy. I shall probably not attain these two attributes even in that world to which the gallows will elevate me in a week or a fortnight's time.

A SHOT

RŮŽENA SVOBODOVÁ

HE often tried to remember what had been
the beginning of it. There was first the
silence of long, uneventful years : days of
no importance, months without incidents, a
passionate longing for life, for something to
happen. Sometimes life begins in this way,
sometimes it ends thus. For him it had been
ordained that the day on which a strange
thing happened should become the first of
many strange days.

The beginning of it had been an early spring
day with all the rested impulses ready to break
forth and spring up ; when the earth opens
her bosom, and yesterday's rain clothes the
fields in their first pale green.

It was a Sunday. Martin, the under-
forester, walking up the hillside behind his
lodge, met Jurko the fool, who was coming
down from somewhere in the hills. His real
name was Jurek Prohabác, and as a rule he
was to be found preaching sermons to the

children on their way home from school. The
forester said : ' Hope you're well, Jurko ? '
He answered : ' Thank you.'

' Looking for rabbit-food ? '

Jurko began to tremble.

' I'm not looking for rabbit-food . . . I'm
not looking for rabbit-food,' he stammered,
then added anxiously : ' I'm looking for traps,
they've been laying traps here.'

Jurko had flashes of clairvoyance in his
muddled head. When there had been theft
or incendiarism, his instinct invariably told
him who was the culprit. This sense in him
seemed to have been developed at the expense
of all the others.

Martin the forester knew that Jurko was
scenting poachers.

The head-forester had gone into the town
early on this Sunday morning, leaving Martin
in charge. Sunday mornings were a favourite
time with the poachers, and Martin was interested in his work, and ambitious. There were
constant little skirmishes between him and the
poachers ; he was ruthless, and they knew it
and hated him ; but no serious incident had
occurred so far. Neither had they, according to
their custom, thrown him bound and gagged into
an anthill, nor had he wounded any of them.

He had his eyes particularly on Flandara, a cunning poacher, who considered the forests his private property, and resented all punishment as an injustice. Whenever he was sentenced to a few months' imprisonment, he would sigh and say : ' All right ! I shall saw logs for the magistrate during the winter and read the Bible from cover to cover. Then I shall go home.'

And when he went home he continued to poach and steal wood. Martin, when he met him, would say to him : ' Your neck has grown quite crooked with looking for crooked firs.'

When you looked for Flandara in the woods, he would be fishing in all the weirs with his flat-bottomed boat full of fish. When you looked on the river-banks he was shooting cartloads of hares in the woods. The Archduke himself once watched him at the station, sending off a consignment of hares. He said ironically that he hoped Flandara had at least shot half of that waggon-load himself.

And Flandara bowed respectfully and said : ' Begging your Grace's pardon, but half of them have been eaten by the magistrates. I had shot twice as many.'

This facetious poacher annoyed Martin, and

he had been longing for some time to put his
mark upon him and make him innocuous.

He was glad he had met Jurko. Perhaps
he would now be able to come to grips with
the satirist. He quietly went in the direction
whence Jurko the fool had come.

Heavy clouds were hanging low above the
forest, the air was full of early spring scents.
The earth's eternal youth was intoxicating him,
and setting his blood on fire. He was thirsting
for life, for action. Men's thirst for action,
for something to do, is ever unquenchable.

Martin's thirst was to shoot at a soft human
body, to cause suffering, to deal retribution.

' You wait ! ' he hissed through his teeth.
He felt as if he had already got hold of the
rascal who always escaped him as by a miracle.

He had reached the path which skirted the
hill like a ring. He carried his gun in his hand
and stooped low, as though on the scent of
the poacher's traces underneath the thick
pine boughs.

Something suddenly stirred in the thicket
without a sound.

' There ! '

Two hands, two powerful hands were
knotting a sling.

' At last ! '

He took aim at the hands and shot.

' Jesus Mary ! '

There was a terrified cry of a tormented human being. Martin the forester jumped into the thick undergrowth. The boughs were lashing his face, he had difficulty in making headway.

He pentrated to the spot where the trap had been laid ; he hoped to find Flandara at the point of death, but he found—nothing. He looked for a track and found blood-stained moss, and a trail of blood which stopped abruptly. He beat about the under-growth in every direction without coming upon any one.

He spent the whole morning in the woods, impatient, annoyed, disappointed. He grew more and more dissatisfied with himself, he could not say why.

His desire had been to hurt, wound, cripple a human being. He had nursed this desire the whole morning, had hardly been able to bide his time. Then he had had his quarry at bay, had wounded a man who had lost so much blood that he was likely to bleed to death somewhere in the bushes ; his lust for blood and murder had been satisfied. And now his teeth were chattering, and the feeling of dissatisfaction was growing stronger and stronger. His chest was beginning to hurt. He threw his gun down, sighed, shook himself, then took the gun up again and went on.

He was a tall fellow, almost a giant, with a small head of dark hair; his eyes usually looked a little dim, and he never quite knew his own mind. Whatever he decided to do, he was always sorry afterwards that he had missed doing the other thing.

He did not go back to his dinner at the forester's house, but went down into the village. He knew he would meet his companion there, the under-forester from the next beat. He felt a need for talk and for a good, deep draught.

As soon as he came into the village, he met Flandara by the first cottage. He was perfectly sound, and bowed to him with the irony of the ever evasive. His smile was condescending and at the same time sarcastic, and his politeness that of a rich peasant bowing to the squire who is head over ears in debt to him. Martin had no feeling of relief.

' Faugh ! ' he ejaculated, and shook himself as he passed the poacher. He went into the inn. His friend, the black forester, was sitting alone at a table in the parlour. Not even the innkeeper was there. Martin threw himself on the seat beside the forester Ernest.

' I have killed a man,' he said and let his head drop heavily forward on his arms.

*   *   *   *   *

The two friends searched the woods all that afternoon for the dead poacher. They found no one. The bloodstains on the moss had became clotted ; they heard no moans. The place was silent as a cemetery. Martin crept through the bushes on his knees, Ernest had to take him away at last and calm him, for fear of his betraying himself. Darkness had set in, and further search would be useless.

Martin began to brood. He tried to understand the complex of feelings which had led to the shot. What had he been thinking of before it happened ? Was there any inevitableness about it ? Had it been necessary for him to take human life ? If only Jurko had not come along ! He hated the sniffing fool, he could have found it in his heart to take his life at this moment, and atone for one murder with another. He

wished he could throw Jurko into the bloody
track of the poacher, so that he should know
what had come of his omniscient babbling, and
suck up and get thoroughly saturated with the
evil consequences of it. He had a bad night.
He went to sleep, but was startled by a dream.
Some one was stepping on his heart, penetrating
his chest. He tried to realize what it was that
was hurting him, and found that a block of
wood with a plank across it was standing on
his chest. On the two ends of the see-saw
were Jurko the fool and a man without a head.
The blood was streaming down over his coat.
They went on perpetually see-sawing, and
each wanted to go higher than the other.
Why must they put this plaything on top of
his chest ?

Jurko was crying : ' Rabbit-food, rabbit-
food ! ' and cackling his thin, wise, old-man's
cackle.

He was sure it had been Jurko who had
brought it all about, because he knew everything and could see into the future ; he had
known exactly how he would set impulse
after impulse throbbing in his heart.

Martin awoke and could not go to sleep
again.

' I've killed a man, that's it,' he remembered.

as soon as he was going to doze off. He turned from side to side, his bed seemed red-hot, he got up unrefreshed, unrested, more tired than when he had lain down.

In the morning the beater Kolar came to him. He was a small sinewy fellow with shoulders on which he might have carried large oak trees, had bright-red hair and a matted beard; his face was freckled, his pale eyes full of cunning. He was an old poacher who had been taken into the service solely to make him innocuous. The expression of his deeply-lined face was restless and vindictive.

He accosted Martin and said spitefully: ' Sir, Novák's old woman from Zbozi has bought six kreutzers' worth of yeast. The old fellow must be in a bad way. Else paupers like that would never buy so much yeast.'

' What has happened to him ? ' asked the forester.

' Don't ask me ; how should I know ? But what does a poacher use yeast for, except his wounds ? ' concluded the red-haired beater.

Martin went to see his friend.

' The man I have wounded is dying. It is old Novák from Zbozi. Tell me, what made me do it ? I have thought about it all night.'

' Don't be a fool,' said his companion. ' You must look unconcerned, so that no one suspects you. We will walk over to Zbozi this afternoon, go to the inn and sit down to drink a glass of beer. Then we shall hear what is the matter with Novák ; no one will dream of fastening the guilt on to you, when they see that you are not afraid of coming down to the village.'

They went. On the way Martin was talking continually under his breath

' Can you explain this passionate desire that I felt to shoot Flandara ? I seemed to be adding to it bit by bit, like a man who piles up coin upon coin of a hoard. I simply had to shoot. I did not keep this passion in check, and now it hurts. I wish I could understand it.'

Ernest the forester said : ' I think you have gone crazy ! Where is the difference between shooting a stag or a poacher ? I could sooner be sorry for a stag, for he is a king, but what is a poacher ? Vermin, common vermin ! There was a whole tribe of poachers in my district. They were living in lonely cottages, and no one could lay their hands on them.

The magistrate had more respect for them than he had for the beaters. He would say : " Sit down, Jansky, the beater may stand."

' We didn't know how to help ourselves. We called in the police, and they surrounded the cottage. No Jansky to be found. We waited until the morning. At break of day some one crept down the ladder. I took aim. Jansky never made a sound, and escaped into the woods. We had a drive, as if we were shooting game. We found him near the pond. He lay like 'a wounded animal. He recovered ; they gave him two months, then he came back, and the whole farce began all over again.

' We were all agreed that we must help ourselves. So he disappeared. The beaters used to tell everybody that Jansky could not be found, neither on the earth nor in the water nor in the air, and they would chuckle.

' But his wife had a little pointer, and she went out to track her husband day and night, but could not find him.

' When at last she came to the fringe of the forest, she found a charred place on the ground. The little pointer stood still and would not stir. It was true, Jansky was to be found neither on the earth nor in the water nor in the air, and yet this little dog had found him. But what evidence can a little dog give? You have been lucky, and ought to be glad. You have shot a fox, and no one can prove that it was you who did it.'

This example failed to raise Martin's spirits. He felt a great loathing for man-killing man.

' Men are beasts,' he murmured between his teeth, ' beasts ! '

They were drawing near to the village.

The young buds of the willows were pressing towards the light, and the trees bent over the mirror of the water, as if they could not gaze enough at their own beauty. The waterfowl were darting hither and thither on the river as though they were intoxicated; children's shouts came from afar. And with all this young, warm, spring atmosphere there was a sound in the air, broken and weary, but persistent—the tolling of the knell. ' The knell,' quaked Martin and ducked involuntarily, as if a breaker were going to swamp him.

The bell rattled on, it sounded like a broken piece of crockery. Martin remembered his dream, when the unknown corpse and Jurko Prohabác were see-sawing on his heart. They seemed to be calling out with nasal voices: ' Ding dong, ding dong.'

Ernest the forester pulled him up sharp :
' Cheer up, every one will get suspicious ! '

They met the red-haired beater near the inn ;
he smiled a sly, knowing smile which wrinkled
up his freckled face till it looked quite small ;
he winked, drew up a corner of his mouth
which usually drooped with continual smoking,
and said : ' Sir, they are not tolling for old
Novák.' He fluttered the fingers of his right
hand in front of his eyes, and the full flavour
of his plebeian, satanic nature came out in
his cackle : ' it's old Háta Látalová who is
dead.'

What irony, spite and superiority there was
in those words ! How they pointed to the
red-haired one's past ! They revealed all
the cautiousness and danger of a poacher's
life, which is never safe for a moment, and yet
he continually gets the better of his pursuers
and daily has his laugh at them.

' What is it to me who is dead ? I don't
know Háta Látalová,' curtly answered Martin
and went into the inn.

When he bade good-morning to the innkeeper, he found that his voice had regained
its usual power. He ordered two glasses of
beer for himself and drank alternately from
both ; he gave a penny to a poor child. Then

he proposed to Ernest that they should sing
a song, and they sang :

> ' 'Neath the limes, above the limes, the lights are
> twinkling,'

and

> ' See the white steed running by the river.'

The red-haired beater came in and sat
down near the door, looking as self-satisfied
as a successful producer of a play. Martin
treated him to as much brandy as he
would like to have. He sat and sipped it
thoughtfully like a connoisseur. The innkeeper went across the parlour to him. He
did not presume to sit down with the gentle-
men.

' How is Novák ? ' the beater asked him.
The tone of his voice left Martin no doubt that
the question was pointed at him, but the
beater had not looked in his direction. The
youth trembled and pushed his glass away
in his confusion.

' He has had the last sacrament,' answered
the innkeeeper, ' but perhaps he may pull
through all the same.'

Martin's melancholy returned. He had
been feeling so happy ! As if old Háta
Látalová had been doing all the dying for

Novák, and his conscience had been cleared;
as though because Háta had died he had
never shot a man, nor felt the desire to murder
Flandara!

The weary sadness which had made him go
to the village, accompanied him through many
days, and roused him from his sleep with the
monotonous call: ' You have killed a man! '

His companion's reiterations of the stories
of poachers killed with the butt end of a rifle
and burnt, did not contribute to his happiness.

Three bad weeks passed; Martin was
suffering. The red-haired beater kept an
obstinate silence. He sometimes eyed Martin
with a half respectful, half ironical look, as
though he were about to tell him the remaining
chapters of the story, then turned away as if
he had changed his mind, and said nothing.

' Were you going to speak to me? ' Martin
would ask in a dull tone of voice

' *I*? Not at all. What could I have to
tell you, sir? ' the beater would answer in
feigned astonishment.

Martin went to Zbozi on his own account.
He went into the inn, and on entering the
parlour said: ' Good-morning,' in a general
way. A guest was sitting at a table in the

corner; he did not return the salutation.
This surprised Martin; he looked up and saw
that it was the poacher, restored to health.

Instantly Martin felt as if his stature were
being raised; strain and torment burst away
from around his heart, which had been encircled as with iron rings. And there was in
this liberated heart a masterful, unsubdued,
high-handed spirit.

'Why don't you answer me?' he shouted
at Novák.

He was pleased to hear his own loud, clear
voice. He had murdered no man; what need
was there to change anything in his ways?

Novák answered him in a cold and sad voice:
'You know quite well why I did not answer
you.'

'How should I know? I have done you
no harm,' lied the youth.

'I have been laid up,' said Novák. 'This
is the first time I have come down here. And
my foot will never be right. The likes of us
don't go to the doctor or the hospital, and
you've splintered the bone and made me a
cripple for life. And all because a poor man
wanted his share from the rich. I love the
woods as much as you do.'

He got up and went towards the door,

dragging his bandaged leg. 'I won't stop in the room with you,' he said, 'I can't answer for myself. But some day we shall have a reckoning. You had no business to make a cripple of me.'

He left the room.

*　　*　　*　　*　　*

No one besides Martin had heard this conversation. It reverberated in his soul like a knell; it took away his joy in life. Sometimes he thought of other things, but he never forgot. He felt like a man who conceals a guilty deed of which he will reap the fruits some day. He lived in anticipation of this, and always went out alone. He was not afraid. A sweet humility had taken possession of him, and sometimes his arms would droop by his side with the poignancy of an obstinately recurring resolve. Some day, when he should meet Novák alone in the solitude of the woods he would say to him : 'I am not going to defend myself—shoot ! '

He wanted to get even with him, to wipe out the impression which the sorrowful voice had left on his soul when it said : 'You had no business to shoot at me—you had no business to make me a cripple.'

Sometimes his soul would melt as though a

spring-sun were thawing it. And when he asked himself whence this feeling came, he discovered that it was caused by this same silent longing to be face to face with the man he had injured so badly ; to deliver himself up to his justice. He knew he was looking forward to this terrible retribution, and that the desire for it made his life more beautiful, made it festal. If it were taken away from him, he would lose that which was sweetest and best in him, and his life would lose its object.

*   *   *   *   *

Autumn came ; following on a summer which Martin had exclusively dedicated to this strange inward experience.

The Archduke came with the young princesses, and they hunted every day. At night they dined at the forester's house, and the foresters went to the inn. Martin was never alone. Words, curses, laughter, and song fell upon his soul, overlaying all that there was in it of sweetness and justice. He longed for solitude, regretted every moment which was stolen from his silent self-examination and sacrificed to other people.

There was a day in October when a warm, soft grey mist lay over the landscape like a

pearl-coloured sea. The sun, although unable to penetrate to its depth, now and then
reached the small windows of the cottages,
and made them sparkle like diamonds.

Towards evening the mist became blood-
red, and through it waded the sickle of the
moon, and bent its wan light over the red
waves of the rapid river. In the course of
the drive Martin had become separated
from the rest of the party, and found himself isolated on a lonely outpost. Perhaps
he had more or less unconsciously sought it ;
perhaps some inward power, stronger than
reason, had led him to it. The cries of the
beaters could not be heard in this place, only
the distant shots. Martin was walking along
a woodland path by the side of a clearing,
which was filled with masses of large anemone
leaves with white, silky fringes. The wind
was swaying them, and the leaves were nodding
obstinately, craning their necks, as though
they were persuading some one, and repeating
with a spiteful pugnacity : ' No, no, no, no ! '

Martin stood still and looked at them.

' God knows why that family has settled
in just that spot,' he murmured. Two hares
ran across the path ; he did not shoot, he
took no interest in them. His eyes followed

them mechanically and rested on the place where they had disappeared.

Suddenly something in his breast leaped up : surely some one was dogging his foot-steps ! It could not be one of the foresters or beaters—impossible. It was a face he knew well, both in reality and in his dreams; he saw it more often than he wished. It was the pale face of Novák.

The poacher's leg was still swathed in rags, it had not healed properly ; he was thin and emaciated.

He was creeping after Martin, but he had no gun. Was he stealing about here for love of the forests and the excitement of the hunt, or was he shadowing him ? Eager to avail himself of the chance which he had demanded of fate, Martin said : ' Novák, what are you doing here ? '

His tone was kind and humble.

Novák did not answer. Martin went up to him with his gun in his hand. Novák gave him a scornful glance.

' You owe me a debt,' said Martin, ' and you have the right to pay it in my own coin. Look here, there is no one within earshot, no one will see or hear us. You have no gun, take mine and shoot.'

He put his gun down at the poacher's feet, stepped back a few paces, leant his back against a tree and waited.

Novák stood motionless, he grew paler still, his eyes glowed with a dull, smouldering fire. He stooped slowly and picked up the gun ; he held it in his hand, weighing it greedily and cunningly without taking his eyes off Martin's face. Martin knew that now at last the moment for simple, natural justice had arrived. He had crippled this man, had meant to murder him, and now the man would settle up with him. Martin had been asking for this ten times daily.

Novák was still standing and weighing the gun in his hands ; only his jaw was working, and his terrible, far-off, sorrowful look searched the forester's face, to try and understand from his expression what he meant. ' Why the devil don't you shoot ? ' cried Martin. His teeth were chattering in short spasms, as if he were in a fever. He was hungering for the shot, but he could hardly bear the delay, and the poacher's irony was not a part of his programme and the whole composition.

' Young Martin, you think I'll be generous and spare you, but what if I do shoot ? You'd better say good-bye to the world. I've been shadowing you, and here you are. What did it matter that I was without a gun? I had only to whistle and my comrades would come; they have guns enough and to spare. Who thinks anything of a shot more or less to-day? There are hundreds of shots; no one will lay the guilt at my door. One of the foresters might easily have done it; the Archduke himself might have been graciously pleased to make a hole in your precious forehead. Who will say it was I? You made a cripple of me. You are right, it is my turn now.' He raised the gun slowly and aimed.

Martin's expression grew hard. An icy line appeared round his lips; his face looked tired and disappointed. Every word Novák had said had annoyed him. He was longing for purity of feeling, rebirth of soul, if need be at the cost of his life; but Novák's talk had been low.

He had been mistaken in his antagonist.

But the poacher too, his keen eyes and his receptive faculties sharpened, when he saw that droop in the corners of the youth's lips, realized that Martin had not counted on being spared, and was every moment getting more disgusted and sorry not to have saved his feelings for some one better, more worthy of them.

His head drooped. In his breast also something was beginning to thaw; that festal feeling was warming his heart and taking him above himself. He said: ' For God's sake, forgive me ! ' and threw the gun into the field of nodding anemones. They were still obstinately repeating: ' No, no, no, no ! ' although no one minded them.

Martin knew from the new light which had come into the poacher's eyes, from the humble droop of his head and the sweetness of his tone, that he had understood. He said: ' You too forgive me, for God's sake.' He held out his hand to him. The poacher drew near. They clasped hands in a firm strong grip. The tears they could have wept, the tenderness of an embrace, were enclosed in this pressure of their hands.

' Have you forgiven me ? ' asked Martin with relief in his voice.

' I have forgiven you.'

Another pressure of their hands, and they parted. The poacher disappeared in the bushes.

Martin took a deep breath and returned to the earth from a strange sphere in which he had been living, returned to a more beautiful earth.

He remembered that he was on duty, and that he was late and would be missed. He picked up his gun and took a short cut through the bushes. Damp clay seemed to hold his steps.

The thick growth of rusty brown leaves, hips, alders, syringas, and young maples hid the distant view.

Martin was not thinking of what he saw, he was looking towards the sky which had cleared. The sun was shining through the beeches, laying pale patches of light at his feet, and touching his burning face.

He felt the warmth and was glad of it ; then he realized that he was humming a tune ; he had not done that since the spring ! And, although his chest was still hurting him, he sang aloud.